Theatre in the Secondary School Classroom

Methods and Strategies for the Beginning Teacher

Jim Patterson, Donna McKenna-Crook,
and Melissa Swick

HEINEMANN
Portsmouth, NH

Heinemann
A division of Reed Elsevier Inc.
361 Hanover Street
Portsmouth, NH 03801-3912
www.heinemanndrama.com

Offices and agents throughout the world

The authors and publisher wish to thank those who have generously given permission to reprint borrowed material:

"Five areas that students should know" from the *National Standards for Arts Education,* published by Music Educators National Conference (MENC). Copyright © 1994 by MENC. Reprinted with permission. The complete National Standards and additional materials relating to the Standards are available from MENC–The National Association for Music Education, 1806 Robert Fulton Drive, Reston, VA 20191 (www.menc.org).

"AATE Theatre Content and Achievement Standards for Grades 5–8 and 9–12." Published by the American Alliance for Theatre and Education. Reprinted by permission of the publisher.

Library of Congress Cataloging-in-Publication Data
Patterson, Jim (Jim Arís)
    Theatre in the secondary school classroom : methods and strategies for the beginning teacher / Jim Patterson, Donna McKenna-Crook, and Melissa Swick.
        p. cm.
    Includes bibliographical references and index.
    ISBN-13: 978-325-00879-0
    ISBN-10: 0-325-00879-5
    1. Theater—Study and teaching (Secondary)—United States. I. McKenna-Crook, Donna. II. Swick, Melissa. III. Title.
PN2078.U6P38 2006
792.071'273—dc22   2006013046

Editor: Lisa A. Barnett
Production editor: Sonja S. Chapman
Cover design: Joni Doherty
Compositor: Valerie Levy / Drawing Board Studios
Manufacturing: Steve Bernier

Printed in the United States of America on acid-free paper
10   09   08   07   06   VP   1   2   3   4   5

Contents

- The Teacher and the School
  Extension Activities
  Stay Connected
  Helpful Hints

6 The Teacher and School Productions—Philosophical Considerations: Building Bridges 104

- Find Out What's Happened Before
- Your Production Philosophy
- Involve Students
- Censorship
- Long-Range Plans for the School Theatre Program
- Revisit Your Choices
  Extension Activities
  Stay Connected
  Helpful Hints

7 The Teacher and School Productions—Practical Considerations: Doing the Job 117

- Work with the Arts Coordinator
- Copyright Considerations
- Space Considerations
- Scheduling Considerations
- Financial and Other Resource Considerations
- Directing Considerations
  Extension Activities
  Stay Connected
  Helpful Hints

8 Resources for the Theatre Teacher: Discovering the Possible 133

- Classroom Materials
- Professional Organizations
- Books, Journals, and Related Sources
- Community Resources
  Extension Activities
  Stay Connected
  Helpful Hints

Preface

Theatre in the Secondary School Classroom is crafted specifically for the prospective theatre teacher who is enrolled in a one-semester teaching methods course. It is intended also for those theatre professionals who are engaged to teach on an emergency or critical needs basis; although these professional theatricians clearly know theatre, they may not know their way around a classroom or a secondary school. We hope that teachers who are completing their first or second year of secondary school teaching will also find much to engage them in *Theatre in the Secondary School Classroom: Methods and Strategies for the Beginning Teacher.* We use the term *secondary school* to mean middle and high school.

Our approach is not to cover everything a new theatre teacher should know; *Theatre in the Secondary School Classroom* is not an encyclopedic work. We believe we have selected for inclusion the cogent areas of inquiry that are a *must* for the beginner.

The beginning theatre teacher will benefit, in short, from an introduction to methods, issues, and strategies that are associated with secondary education in a broader sense, as well as specific topics that are particular to teaching theatre. This text endeavors to provide useful tools in both of these areas—the theoretical as well as the practical. Our particular goal, then, is to extend accepted theory to specific classroom practice. Clearly, *Theatre in the Secondary School Classroom* emphasizes the practical aspects of secondary theatre classroom teaching.

The three authors of this text have taught theatre in middle and high schools for a combined total of thirty-three years, and have taught in university and college theatre programs for forty-seven years, frequently working with students preparing to teach theatre themselves. Although our combined experience encompasses several careers, we continue to learn new things about teaching theatre. This book presents what we feel will be useful tools for educators beginning to teach theatre in middle and high school settings; it is intended to be one resource among many that a teacher gathers throughout a career.

Philosophical Overview

One significant philosophical underpinning of *Theatre in the Secondary School Classroom* is that the new teacher should always link the school play production program to classroom learning. We believe play production is a laboratory for learning the intricacies of theatre arts. In short, we believe play production is to theatre arts what the biology lab is to the biological sciences.

We also have a clear belief that play production programs should be student-centered. As such, we place emphasis on student-written, student-directed, student-designed, and student-managed productions. That means, for us, theatre production must include more than the study and performance of formal play scripts. Theatre reaches beyond traditional study of dramatic literature, theatre history, and production techniques to incorporate student-centered learning, in which theatre is generated from and made by the young people themselves.

The beginning teacher is encouraged to take a broad, inquisitive view of what it means to experience theatre in the classroom. We believe effective theatre classrooms will empower and engage young people in a multi-faceted exploration of theatrical forms and meanings.

Features

Theatre in the Secondary School Classroom incorporates a number of features that we hope will appeal to both teachers and students. They include the following.

> ➤ **Each Chapter Is Theatre-Specific** Every illustration, work example, rubric, test question, and the like comes from the discipline of theatre.

> ➤ **Three Unique Features Conclude Each Chapter** Extension Activities suggest ways to help future teachers explore the subject. Some are phrased as homework assignments, if the instructor wishes to use them as such. Stay Connected cites Web addresses that can provide additional resource and research

materials that expand upon the chapter topics. Helpful Hints provide suggestions for success that the new theatre teacher might consider adopting.

➤ **Easy Reading** We've encapsulated appropriate material in bulleted checklists and listings. These materials break up the text yet call typographical attention to important issues and questions facing new educators.

➤ **Conciseness** Although we believe we have covered basic material that every young theatre teacher should know, we have relied on the virtue of succinctness.

➤ **Sample Materials** The appendix contains model letters to parents about course requirements, requirements for actors who are cast in a school production, and the like.

Two Suggestions

We believe that each student enrolled in a theatre methods course should be asked to keep a resource portfolio of materials produced during the semester. Anytime future teachers prepare an assignment for this course, it should be duplicated for each member of the class. These materials might include lesson plans, sample assessment items, and the like. Each student should be required to surf the web for appropriate materials, which are then included in the resource portfolio. (See Stay Connected found at the end of each chapter.) We have included in Appendix C a model rubric (that the professor is welcome to use and modify) for guidance and assessment for the resource portfolio. If this assignment is made at the beginning of the course, then students will have a bank of materials that they will find useful during those crucial first years of teaching.

Each chapter is independent of the one that precedes it or follows it. We have arranged them in an order that was influenced by the dozens of theatre methods class syllabi that we consulted in the research stage of this book. That is, our arrangement of chapters coincides with the way various college and university instructors have organized this material for their own classrooms. However, if it is more convenient for the instructor to assign chapters in a different sequence, you have our blessing. We believe, for example, that the chapter on integrated teaching across the curriculum (Chapter 5) could be assigned earlier than it appears or it could be assigned as the final reading.

Good Luck

The beginning teacher, no matter what the field, does not enter the profession as a fully developed educator—indeed, teachers with many years of experience often view themselves as works in progress. As you navigate the first few years of teaching, you will make valuable discoveries about yourself as an educator and about the field of theatre education. We wrote this book in an effort to help guide the first steps of a journey.

Acknowledgments

We are deeply indebted to Professors Patti P. Gillespie, Norma T. Ragsdale, Kevin Swick, Sara Nalley, and Elbin Cleveland who read early drafts of this text. We sincerely thank three teachers, Leslie Dellinger, Sue Swick, and Shannon Reed, whose feedback on later drafts was invaluable. Their insights have added greatly to the organization, content, and clarity of *Theatre in the Secondary School Classroom.*

Professor Patterson learned much about what "worked" in the classroom (and what didn't!) when he used a late draft of this book to teach the theatre methods course at the University of South Carolina in Fall 2005. His students helped him suggest revisions to his coauthors (who readily embraced the suggestions and corrections). Thus we are beholden to Angel Borths, David Donelan, Tori Jepson, Quesha Lyles, Myra Shaffer, Genevieve Sloan, and Stephanie Walker for their considered classroom feedback.

All of the charts, checklists, examples, and rubrics found within these chapters are the work of the authors. We are pleased that the National Music Educators gave us permission to reprint the "Five Basic Areas of Knowledge" section found in Chapter 1.

We thank Jimmy Flannery for the inventive classroom procedures found in Chapter 3. The model correspondence found in the appendix was written by Donna McKenna-Crook and Melissa Swick and adapted for use here. Ms. McKenna-Crook dedicates her contribution to this book to her three children, Jessica, Justin, and Chelsea, from whom she has learned everything that really matters.

1

National Theatre Standards
American Arts Instruction Undergoes a Radical Change

Theatre study offers the student a unique educational experience. It involves literature but it is not a course in English or language arts. Theatre education includes an examination of the history of other times and places but it is not a course in world history. Theatre involves physical activity and group undertakings but it is not physical education. Theatre explores human psychology, concerns the construction of physical objects, involves public performance, and practices critical valuing. Theatre study can be seen as an exploration of personal self-expression, as well as the study of an art form. In short, theatre offers a way to explore the world around us as well as worlds from other times and places.

Because theatre is such a complex field of study, it's fortunate that beginning teachers have major resources on which to draw: the national theatre content and achievement standards. During the 1990s the K–12 curriculum in American schools underwent a revolution when, in 1992, The National Council on Education Standards and Testing requested that all disciplines develop voluntary national standards. This call meant that all subject areas were to develop, independently and through consensus, content standards as well as achievement standards. That is, the standards should describe what students should know and what students should be able to do.

The National Endowment for the Arts and the U.S. Department of Education granted to the Music Educators National Conference, now called the National Association for Music Education, a little over one million dollars to develop voluntary national standards for each arts discipline—music, theatre, dance, and the visual arts. From these standards arts curricula could be developed.

The Consortium of National Arts Education Associations supervised the standards project for the arts. Theatre standards were developed through the aegis of the American Alliance for Theatre and Education (AATE) by calling together respected theatre artists, educators, and consultants. A draft of the standards this group developed was distributed to arts consultants, selected members of the consortium, other theatre educators, and AATE constituents. Based on the responses from these sources, the theatre standards were honed, clarified, and revised more than once. A consensus eventually was forged. By March 1994 the completed arts standards were presented to the U.S. Secretary of Education.

During the latter half of the 1990s, various states adopted these standards. Some states made gentle modifications in the national standards when they were adopted. By 2002, according to one national survey, forty states had adopted a form of the national standards devised by the AATE. However, even those eleven states that had not endorsed the standards were influenced by the strength and momentum of the National Arts Standards movement.

Once a particular state endorsed the content and achievement standards, curricula could then be developed for all grade levels that would lead the state to meet the eight theatre standards. The brilliance of the standards approach is that it does not dictate curricula; states have the autonomy to design their own curricula and courses. By describing outcomes not methodology, the national theatre standards leave room for the states to address local constraints and needs and for theatre teachers to respond to local traditions and individual student capabilities.

Theatre education all over America is now influenced by the standards developed over a decade ago. Theatre teachers, therefore, must know these national standards as well as the standards their particular state has developed. Because the standards help define what a good theatre education should provide, curricula in most school districts have been developed to meet these standards. In sum, the theatre standards, as well as those in the other arts, bring a rigor to the arts disciplines.

Five Basic Areas of Knowledge

The standards in each arts discipline were devised to cover five major areas of understanding. According to the Consortium of National Arts Education Associations, students should be able to:

> ➤ Communicate at a basic level in the four arts disciplines—dance, music, theatre, and the visual arts. This includes knowledge

and skills in the use of the basic vocabularies, materials, tools, techniques, and intellectual methods of each arts discipline.

➤ Communicate proficiently in at least one art form, including the ability to define and solve artistic problems with insight, reason, and technical proficiency.

➤ Develop and present basic analyses of works of art from structural, historical, and cultural perspectives and from the combinations of those perspectives. This includes the ability to understand and evaluate work in the various arts disciplines.

➤ Demonstrate an informed acquaintance with exemplary works of art from a variety of cultures and historical periods, and a basic understanding of historical development in the arts disciplines, across the arts as a whole and within cultures.

➤ Relate various types of arts knowledge and skills within and across the arts disciplines. This includes mixing and matching competencies and understandings in art making, history and culture, and analysis in any arts-related project.

One important consequence of the national standards movement is that it obligates theatre teachers to broaden their teaching to include other areas of the fine arts by drawing comparisons and references to art, music, dance, and the visual arts when teaching about theatre in any era. Because of the standards movement, theatre teachers must not treat theatre as an isolated art form; connectivity to the other fine arts is now required.

Theatre Standards for Grades Five through Eight

In theatre, the artists create an imagined world about human beings; it is the role of the actor to lead the audience into the visual, aural, and oral world. To help students in grades 5–8 develop theatre literacy, it is important that they learn to see the created world of theatre through the eyes of the playwright, actor, designer, and director. Through active creation of theatre, students learn to understand artistic choices and to critique dramatic works. Students should, at this point, play a larger role in the planning and evolution of their work. They should continue to use drama as a means of confidently expressing their worldview, thus developing their "personal voice." The drama should also introduce students to plays that reach beyond their communities to national, international, and historically representative themes.

Content Standard #1: Script writing by the creation of improvisations and scripted scenes based on personal experience and heritage, imagination, literature, and history

Achievement Standard

➤ Students individually and in groups, create characters, environments, and actions that create tension and suspense.

➤ Students refine and record dialogue and action.

Content Standard #2: Acting by developing basic acting skills to portray characters who interact in improvised and scripted scenes

Achievement Standard

➤ Students analyze descriptions, dialogue, and actions to discover, articulate, and justify character motivation and invent character behaviors based on the observation of interactions, ethical choices, and emotional responses of people.

➤ Students demonstrate acting skills (such as sensory recall, concentration, breath control, diction, body alignment, control of isolated body parts) to develop characterizations that suggest artistic choices.

➤ Students in an ensemble, interact as the invented characters.

Content Standard #3: Designing by developing environments for improvised and scripted scenes

Achievement Standard

➤ Students explain the functions and interrelated nature of scenery, properties, lighting, sound, costumes, and makeup in creating an environment appropriate for the drama.

➤ Students analyze improvised and scripted scenes for technical requirements.

➤ Students develop focused ideas for the environment using visual elements (line, texture, color, space), visual principles (repetition, balance, emphasis, contrast, unity), and aural qualities (pitch, rhythm, dynamics, tempo, expression) from traditional and nontraditional sources.

➤ Students work collaboratively and safely to select and create elements of scenery, properties, lighting, and sound, to signify environments, and costumes and makeup, to suggest character.

Content Standard #4: Directing by organizing rehearsals for improvised and scripted scenes

Achievement Standard

> ➤ Students lead small groups in planning visual and aural elements and in rehearsing improvised and scripted scenes, demonstrating social, group, and consensus skills.

Content Standard #5: Researching by using cultural and historical information to support improvised and scripted scenes

Achievement Standard

> ➤ Students apply research from print and nonprint sources to script writing, acting, design, and directing choices.

Content Standard #6: Comparing and incorporating art forms by analyzing methods of presentation and audience response for theatre, dramatic media (such as film, television, and electronic media), and other art forms

Achievement Standard

> ➤ Students describe characteristics and compare the presentation of characters, environments, and actions in theatre, musical theatre, dramatic media, dance, and visual arts.
> ➤ Students incorporate elements of dance, music, and visual arts to express ideas and emotions in improvised and scripted scenes.
> ➤ Students express and compare personal reactions to several art forms.
> ➤ Students describe and compare the functions and interaction of performing and visual artists and audience members in theatre, dramatic media, musical theatre, dance, music, and visual arts.

Content Standard #7: Analyzing, evaluating, and constructing meanings from improvised and scripted scenes and from theatre, film, television, and electronic media productions

Achievement Standard

> ➤ Students describe and analyze the effect of publicity, study guides, programs, and physical environments on audience response and appreciation of dramatic performances.

➤ Students articulate and support the meanings constructed from their and others' dramatic performances.

➤ Students use articulated criteria to describe, analyze, and constructively evaluate the perceived effectiveness of artistic choices found in dramatic performances.

➤ Students describe and evaluate the perceived effectiveness of students' contributions to the collaborative process of developing improvised and scripted scenes.

Content Standard #8: Understanding context by analyzing the role of theatre, film, television, and electronic media in the community and in other cultures

Achievement Standard

➤ Students describe and compare universal characters and situations in dramas from and about various cultures and historical periods, illustrate in improvised and scripted scenes, and discuss how theatre reflects a culture.

➤ Students explain the knowledge, skills, and discipline needed to pursue careers and avocational opportunities in theatre, film, television, and electronic media.

➤ Students analyze the emotional and social impact of dramatic events in their lives, in the community, and in other cultures.

➤ Students explain how culture affects the content and production values of dramatic performances.

➤ Students explain how social concepts such as cooperation, communication, collaboration, consensus, self-esteem, risk taking, sympathy, and empathy apply in theatre and daily life.

Theatre Standards for Grades Nine Through Twelve

Note that each standard for grades nine through twelve has two achievement levels; one describes basic proficiency and the other delineates advanced proficiency.

In grades nine through twelve, students view and construct dramatic works as metaphorical visions of life that embrace connotative meanings, juxtaposition, ambiguity, and varied interpretations. By creating, performing, analyzing, and critiquing dramatic performances, they develop a deeper understanding of personal issues and a broader worldview that includes global issues. Since theatre in all its forms reflects and affects life, students should learn about representative dramatic texts and performances and the place of that work and those events in history. Classroom work becomes more formalized with the advanced students participating in theatre, film, television, and electronic media productions.

Content Standard #1: Script writing through improvising, writing, and refining scripts based on personal experience and heritage, imagination, literature, and history

Achievement Standard, Proficient

➤ Students construct imaginative scripts and collaborate with actors to refine scripts so that story and meaning are conveyed to an audience.

Achievement Standard, Advanced

➤ Students write theatre, film, television, or electronic media scripts in a variety of traditional and new forms that include original characters with unique dialogue that motivates action.

Content Standard #2: Acting by developing, communicating, and sustaining characters in improvisations and informal or formal productions

Achievement Standard, Proficient

➤ Students analyze the physical, emotional, and social dimensions of characters found in dramatic texts from various genres and media.

➤ Students compare and demonstrate various classical and contemporary acting techniques and methods.

➤ Students in an ensemble, create and sustain characters that communicate with audiences.

Achievement Standard, Advanced

➤ Students demonstrate artistic discipline to achieve an ensemble in rehearsal and performance.

➤ Students create consistent characters from classical, contemporary, realistic, and nonrealistic dramatic texts in informal and formal theatre, film, television, or electronic media productions.

Content Standard #3: Designing and producing by conceptualizing and realizing artistic interpretations for informal or formal productions

Achievement Standard, Proficient

➤ Students explain the basic physical and chemical properties of the technical aspects of theatre (such as light, color, electricity, paint, and makeup).

➤ Students analyze a variety of dramatic texts from cultural and historical perspectives to determine production requirements.

➤ Students develop designs that use visual and aural elements to convey environments that clearly support the text.

➤ Students apply technical knowledge and skills to collaboratively and safely create functional scenery, properties, lighting, sound, costumes, and makeup.

➤ Students design coherent stage management, promotional, and business plans.

Achievement Standard, Advanced

➤ Students explain how scientific and technological advances have impacted set, light, sound, and costume design and implementation for theatre, film, television, and electronic media productions.

➤ Students collaborate with directors to develop unified production concepts that convey the metaphorical nature of the drama for informal and formal theatre, film, television, or electronic media productions.

➤ Students safely construct and efficiently operate technical aspects of theatre, film, television, or electronic media productions.

➤ Students create and reliably implement production schedules, stage management plans, promotional ideas, and business and front of house procedures for informal and formal theatre, film, television, or electronic media productions.

Content Standard #4: Directing by interpreting dramatic texts and organizing and conducting rehearsals for informal or formal productions

Achievement Standard, Proficient

➤ Students develop multiple interpretations and visual and aural production choices for scripts and production ideas and choose those that are most interesting.

➤ Students justify selections of text, interpretation, and visual and aural artistic choices.

➤ Students effectively communicate directorial choices to a small ensemble for improvised or scripted scenes.

Achievement Standard, Advanced

➤ Students explain and compare the roles and interrelated responsibilities of the various personnel involved in theatre, film, television, and electronic media productions.

➤ Students collaborate with designers and actors to develop aesthetically unified production concepts for informal and formal theatre, film, television, or electronic media productions.

➤ Students conduct auditions, cast actors, direct scenes, and conduct production meetings to achieve production goals.

Content Standard #5: Researching by evaluating and synthesizing cultural and historical information to support artistic choices

Achievement Standard, Proficient

➤ Students identify and research cultural, historical, and symbolic clues in dramatic texts and evaluate the validity and practicality of the information to assist in making artistic choices for informal and formal productions.

Achievement Standard, Advanced

➤ Students research and describe appropriate historical production designs, techniques, and performances from various cultures to assist in making artistic choices for informal and formal theatre, film, television, or electronic media productions.

Content Standard #6: Comparing and integrating art forms by analyzing traditional theatre, dance, music, visual arts, and new art forms

Achievement Standard, Proficient

➤ Students describe and compare the basic nature, materials, elements, and means of communicating in theatre, dramatic media, musical theatre, dance, music, and the visual arts.

➤ Students determine how the nondramatic art forms are modified to enhance the expression of ideas and emotions in theatre.

➤ Students illustrate the integration of several arts media in informal presentations.

Achievement Standard, Advanced

➤ Students compare the interpretive and expressive natures of several art forms in a specific culture or historical period.

➤ Students compare the unique interpretive and expressive natures and aesthetic qualities of traditional arts from various cultures and historical periods with contemporary new art forms (such as performance art).

➤ Students integrate several arts and/or media in theatre, film, television, or electronic media productions.

Content Standard #7: Analyzing, critiquing, and constructing meanings from informal and formal theatre, film, television, and electronic media productions

Achievement Standard, Proficient

➤ Students construct social meanings from informal and formal productions and from dramatic performances from a variety of cultures and historical periods and relate these to current personal, national, and international issues.

➤ Students articulate and justify personal aesthetic criteria for critiquing dramatic texts and events that compare perceived artistic intent with the final aesthetic achievement.

➤ Students analyze and critique the whole and the parts of dramatic performances, taking into account the context, and constructively suggest alternative artistic choices.

➤ Students constructively evaluate their own and others' collaborative efforts and artistic choices in informal and formal productions.

Achievement Standard, Advanced

➤ Students construct personal meanings from nontraditional dramatic performances.

➤ Students analyze, compare, and evaluate differing critiques of the same dramatic texts and performances.

➤ Students critique several dramatic works in terms of other aesthetic philosophies (such as the underlying ethos of Greek drama, French classicism with its unities of time and place, Shakespeare and romantic forms, Indian classical drama, Japanese kabuki, and others).

➤ Students analyze and evaluate critical comments about personal dramatic work explaining which points are most appropriate to inform further development of the work.

Content Standard #8: Understanding context by analyzing the role of theatre, film, television, and electronic media in the past and the present

Achievement Standard, Proficient

➤ Students compare how similar themes are treated in drama from various cultures and historical periods, illustrate with informal performances, and discuss how theatre can reveal universal concepts.

➤ Students identify and compare the lives, works, and influence of representative theatre artists in various cultures and historical periods.

➤ Students identify cultural and historical sources of American theatre and musical theatre.

➤ Students analyze the effect of their own cultural experiences on their dramatic work.

Achievement Standard, Advanced

➤ Students analyze the social and aesthetic impact of under-represented theatre and film artists.

➤ Students analyze the relationships among cultural values, freedom of artistic expression, ethics, and artistic choices in various cultures and historical periods.

➤ Students analyze the development of dramatic forms, production practices, and theatrical traditions across cultures and historical periods and explain influences on contemporary theatre, film, television, and electronic media productions.

If there is some question as to the exact meaning of a particular content standard, then closely examine the achievement standard(s) that follow. The achievement standards embody the particular knowledge the student should be able to demonstrate based on the specific content standard. For example, high school Content Standard #7 is concerned with "analyzing, critiquing, and constructing meaning" in certain media—theatre, film, television, and electronic productions. What, specifically, is the content standard about? A study of the proficient and advanced achievement standards will reveal, rather specifically, what students should be able to do or make.

Key Terms

The theatre content and achievements standards include a number of key terms that the beginning teacher should know. They include: *action, aesthetic criteria, aesthetic qualities, artistic choices, classical, classroom dramatizations, constructed meaning, drama, dramatic media, electronic media, ensemble, environment, formal production, improvisation, informal production, new art forms, role, script, social pretend play, tension, text, theatre, theatre literacy, traditional forms, unified production concept.* Theatre teachers must be conversant with the concepts inherent in these terms as they are integral to understanding the standards.

Significant Changes Demanded

The acceptance of the national arts standards changed the way theatre is taught in American schools. Prior to the enactment of the standards, theatre education usually centered on playwriting, acting, design, directing, and the history of the theatre (including a study of playwrights from past and present). The standards demanded two important changes: Theatre as an art form was to be placed in the context of the fine arts where connections between all of the arts must be made, and the realm of theatre studies was expanded to include popular media.

Theatre teachers in this new millennium, in short, must widen their approach to other fine arts by drawing comparisons and references to the visual arts, music, and dance in all eras, past and present. Theatre teachers must reexamine their definition of theatre to venture beyond live theatre by embracing expressions of theatrical art that are found on the two-dimensional screens of movies, television, and computer games. Even radio, a one-dimensional medium, is included in this expanded definition of theatre. Although three-dimensional live theatre was the predominant dramatic form for centuries, we now live in a media-infused culture where live theatre is but one dramatic expression. The standards require the twenty-first-century theatre teacher to embrace the broadening of the theatre curriculum.

Document the Teaching of Standards in Planning

When courses are devised, lesson plans constructed, and activities identified, the teacher should recognize the content standard(s) being met by making an appropriate notation in the particular document. For example, an "S1" notation would indicate that the activity addresses the "script writing" content standard. We have endeavored to employ this same technique throughout this book. When, for example, this symbol ❼ is associated with an exercise, you know that we believe the exercise addresses Content Standard #7. If two symbols appear, ❷ and ❹ for instance, then the lesson will involve the acting and directing standards.

It will be a rare classroom experience indeed if most *every* content standard is addressed during one single lesson. However, teachers are expected to have developed in their students the appropriate achievement standard level for each content standard by the end of a course. Figure 1–1 represents a summary of the content standards followed by a few classroom activities for each standard. In addition, the numeric dingbats in the extreme right column indicate that a single activity can address more than one content standard.

	Primary Standards	Classroom Activities That Will Address Primary Standards	Other Standards
❶	Script writing	Improvising a scene and then giving literary form to the improv.	❷
❷	Acting	Improvs; scene study; formal and informal performances; create a character scrapbook for central characters in a play being studied that involves given circumstances, back stories.	❶ ❹ ❺ ❼ ❽
❸	Designing	Teams create the environments for a series of preselected plays presented to the class as models using music and visual arts to further communicate the mood of the plays.	❺ ❻ ❼ ❽
❹	Directing	Organizing rehearsals; analyzing scripts for performance	❺ ❼ ❽
❺	Researching	Study of a particular time in theatre history; explore the cultural background of a formal script.	❻ ❽
❻	Comparing and integrating other art forms	Students each research a character from American history; using the character's words, they write a script and provide transitional material; the monodrama is presented with costume and music.	❶ ❷ ❸ ❹ ❺ ❽

	Primary Standards	Classroom activities that will address primary standards	Other Standards
❼	Analyzing, evaluating, and constructing meaning in various media	A student team rehearses and tapes a scene outside of class, another team rehearses the same scene, then both scenes are presented in class. How was meaning constructed? Teacher presents three movie versions of a scene from *Romeo and Juliet*. Class investigates how meaning was communicated.	❷ ❸ ❹ ❺ ❻ ❽
❽	Media in society	Teams select a theme (such as prejudice or fear) and research how these themes are used in plays from other periods. Teams examine five current sitcoms to discover what universal themes they dramatize.	❺ ❻ ❼

Figure 1–1 Study this chart, especially the classroom activities. Can you see how each of the activities addresses the appropriate standard? Why, for example, are the activities that illustrate Standard #7 said to also address six other standards? Bear in mind that the "other standards" in the list above may be addressed through the activities, depending on how the teacher approaches the material. Throughout this book, when specific standards are linked with suggested activities, it is important to remember that the individual teacher's approach to structuring the lesson will determine whether or not the standards are addressed.

EXTENSION ACTIVITIES

1. Using a search engine, locate and print theatre standards for your state and one other state of your choice. As a class compare the downloaded standards to the national standards. Are they similar? How do they differ?

2. Compare the middle school standards with those of grades nine through twelve. As a class, discuss the ways in which the high school content standards build upon the middle school standards.

3. As a class define the terms listed in the Key Terms section of this chapter. Check the definitions given in class with those that can be found in the Stay Connected site.

STAY CONNECTED

Log on to artsedge.kennedy-center.org/teach/standards/contents.cfm and find Appendix A (at the bottom of the opening page), then click on Theatre. Download the Theatre Glossary for definitions of the key terms cited in this chapter. Explore this site to also discover standards for visual arts, dance, and music.

HELPFUL HINTS

➤ **Archive Letters**   Well before the first day of class, set aside a specific file drawer (or box) that can house every scrap of paper that documents your success as a teacher and the success of the program—students' letters, parents' letters, alums' letters, clippings, programs, and reviews. These items can be used in support of the program whether issues be budgetary matters or production planning.

➤ **File Old Materials**   Dedicate another file drawer to house every lesson plan, unit or course plan, test, student handout, checklist, rubric, and other teaching materials that you have prepared. If you keep such items in a computer, be sure to back up your materials and place the disk in this file drawer. Then, in a moment of contemplation you can study a particular item for revision or reuse.

➤ **Keep Reading**   When possible spend at least 30 minutes every other day perusing theatrical periodical literature. Not only will this help keep you informed, it may also stimulate new and useful teaching ideas and uncover timely material that you can share with your students.

➤ **Find a Mentor**   If you are part of a department, the department chair is an excellent resource. New teachers are often assigned a mentor. It is important that you take advantage of this relationship, even if it is to simply stop by and say hello. Set up a reasonable time to meet occasionally to ask advice, but don't make a pest of yourself. Sooner rather than later is your best approach. Small problems are quickly solved.

2

Planning
Think Forward—Plan Backward

Imagine for a moment that you are in the market for a new house. You begin to make a list of the tasks involved, always the first step in making a plan. Your list looks something like this:

- ➤ Attend closing for new house
- ➤ Find new house
- ➤ Have the new house inspected
- ➤ Sell current house
- ➤ Make an offer on the new house
- ➤ Move in to new house
- ➤ Secure financing
- ➤ Pick a real estate agent

Real estate experts agree that these activities are some of the main chores involved in buying a new house. But the endeavors are greatly out of order. Planning is often defined as identifying the tasks necessary to accomplish an objective and arranging those tasks in an effective order. For the house-buying example, one order might be:

- ➤ Pick a real estate agent
- ➤ Find new house
- ➤ Make an offer
- ➤ Have the new house inspected
- ➤ Secure financing

> ➤ Sell current house
> ➤ Attend closing for new house
> ➤ Move in to new house

A better plan would realize that some activities are best conducted simultaneously, such as:

> ➤ Pick a real estate agent
> ➤ Secure financing
> ➤ Sell current house
> ➤ Find new house $\Big\}$ (simultaneous with other activities, not later than "Attend closing")
> ➤ Make an acceptable offer
> ➤ Have the new house inspected
> ➤ Attend closing for new house
> ➤ Move in to new house

As a new home buyer, you have established an efficient plan. You have decided that moving into the new house is your final goal and you have arranged all the other tasks to logically lead to that goal. That is exactly what teachers do when they make plans. They think forward but plan backward.

Planning is, in short, more than just making a schedule. Scheduling puts events into units of available time; planning is scheduling time for events in an order that will effectively and efficiently accomplish a set of goals. In teaching, planning is the answer to the questions: What must the student learn first in order to create the background and foundation for meeting the remainder of the course goals? How much time will each step in the plan take?

Of course, for many plans, the order of steps will not be tightly constrained. That is, the possible order of steps is flexible. In the analogy of house buying above, you can start looking at houses on the market before ever putting your own house up for sale. Other steps are strictly contingent upon one another and can only be performed in one order. For example, one cannot attend the house closing before the loan has been obtained.

Planning is done in every endeavor, from routing the collection of garbage in residential areas to launching the space shuttle. Teaching has its own special language and techniques for planning, which will be explored in this chapter.

School Planning

Planning may be the single most important task for which the teacher is responsible. Skillful planning alone may not ensure a successful teaching career yet without the structure provided by a thoughtful plan, classroom success may be elusive. This is especially true for the new teacher. Planning not only requires the teacher to incorporate all the goals and objectives that are laid out in the mandated curriculum, it also sets the tone of the classroom experience and determines the pace at which the teacher and students will work throughout the term.

A teacher's ability to plan and organize courses, units of instruction within a course, and daily lessons requires serious thought and concentrated, detailed work. Curriculum planning, then, is best done well before the first day of classes. Planning must include both the long term and the short term. It includes the teacher's ability to:

➤ work logically and realistically within a framework that is laid out in the curriculum documentation provided by the school or district

➤ understand as quickly as possible the students' ability levels and interests

➤ devise meaningful learning activities

➤ set realistic expectations

➤ maintain consistency

➤ assimilate and apply the procedural requirements and expectations of the school itself.

The Calendar and Planning

Every teacher must first develop a yearlong calendar that incorporates all the prescribed deadlines set by the school and the district. Such dates include first and last days of classes for each semester, the dates on which report cards are issued, official school holidays, inservice training dates, final exam days, grade submission dates, standardized testing dates, and the like. When this schedule is complete, the teacher will know how many days of actual classroom instruction are available in each semester. Armed with this knowledge, curriculum planning can begin.

The calendar should be further enhanced by inserting established schoolwide activities, including major sporting events, chorus and band concerts, and such activities. When this calendar is finally completed, a fairly comprehensive picture of the semester and school year will emerge. It is within this overview that projects more limited in scope can be addressed. For example, if a full-length play is scheduled to open for three performances in the second week of November, then one must allow six to eight weeks to develop the production, including auditions, rehearsals, and readying the sets and costumes. The play, it follows, must be selected and announced during the first week of September. If the teacher intends to participate in district- and/or statewide dramatic festivals, then these dates must be added to the master calendar.

This master scheduling document, the yearlong calendar, becomes a reference tool for teacher and student alike. Many experienced teachers post this document in their classrooms for all to use.

Curriculum Planning

Effective teachers must be good thinkers as well as good planners. Whether the teacher is planning a course, unit, or individual lesson, four important areas must be considered.

➤ What does the teacher expect the student to know at the end of the experience? These expectations are called *learner objectives.*

➤ What activities will the teacher design to promote student learning?

➤ How will the learner objectives be assessed? That is, how will students be evaluated to determine if both the teacher and the student have been successful in communicating general and specific goals?

➤ Do the assessment procedures match the learner objectives?

➤ Do the learner objectives coincide with the state's content standards?

The answers to these questions require careful thought and advance planning, surely well before the first week of school. The discussion that follows will help you make logical decisions that will enhance classroom learning.

Be clear about what you will assess. Learner objectives can, and must, be specific and capable of being measured either subjectively or objectively within the timeframe of the course. If the teacher maintains, for example, that one learner outcome is that "students should be better able to appreciate the art and craft of acting" once they have completed a semester-long course on acting, then it should be clear that the teacher is obligated to define the phrase *better appreciate.*

This goal, nebulous as it is, can be assessed, if at all, only by observing the behavior of students after they have completed the acting course. The teacher might note, for example, that students regularly attend local theatre productions, they discuss among themselves during leisure hours the pros and cons of the performance of the various actors, they begin to read more plays, they try to learn about famous actors of the past, they act in community theatre productions, or the like.

Clearly, this kind of behavior will take several months or years to observe. Yet grades for the acting course may be due in two weeks. The problem, of course, is contained in the *better appreciate* phrase contained in the learner objectives. It is vague and depends on the teacher observing the student's behavior over a long period of time. Clearly the outcome must be rephrased to make it more specific and capable of being measured.

Consider this restatement of a learner objective for an acting class: "The student will be better able to appreciate the art and craft of acting by

"1. demonstrating during scene and monologue performances the following skills: [name the acting skills you will teach] and by

"2. describing the following concepts and/or terms [name the concepts/terms you will teach]"

These objectives can be measured, the first subjectively by using a performance rubric. The second can be measured effectively by the quality of the written preparation of the performance material and tests requiring an explanation of concepts and/or terms. The beginning teacher will find that *demonstrate* and *describe* are very useful verbs in setting forth what the student should know at the end of the course, the unit, and the lesson. Other useful descriptors to master when writing instructional objectives include *differentiate between, perform, compare and contrast, list,* and *identify.* Avoid general and vague verbs like *know, understand,* and *fully appreciate* unless you specify clearly how you will measure the internal states inherent in these verbs.

Course Planning

The master calendar will reveal the actual number of teaching days in each semester. Armed with this vital information, individual courses can be designed. If, for example, the course is theatre appreciation, then the teacher should make a list of the topics to be covered, how much class time should be devoted to each component, and what the student should know about each area.

A typical list of topics for a theatre appreciation course might include:

➤ the nature and essence of theatre

➤ actor-audience relationships

➤ a survey of theatre art: playwriting, acting, directing, design (sets, costumes, lights, makeup, and sound)

➤ critical response to theatre

➤ the role of the audience

➤ making theatre

The course plan is then expanded by developing a time frame for each topic, a brief topic sentence describing the content, along with some suggestions of the materials and activities that might be used. A sample outline for a one-semester introduction to theatre (or theatre appreciation) course that meets five times a week can be found in Figure 2–1.

Theatre I: Course Plan
**Usually attracts ninth- and tenth-grade students but juniors also elect. Text: *Theatre: Art in Action*
One eighteen-week semester**

➤ **The nature of theatre; theatre and its place among the fine arts—one week**

Because it is live, interactive, and ephemeral, theatre differs from television and movies. Theatre, in its most general considerations, can include, music, dance, visual arts, and opera. ❻

➤ **The essence of theatre—one week**

Like all of the fine arts, theatre is artificial (a "made" thing) yet it aims at "truth." All that is necessary to make theatre is actors, an audience, a place, and an action (event). Improvs to exemplify. ❶ ❻ ❼

➤ **Actor-audience configurations—one week**

How the space is arranged affects the production and the audience. Three arrangements: arena, thrust, proscenium. ❺❻

➤ **Theatre arts—eight weeks**

Theatre is an artistic collaboration between playwright, actors, director, and designers.

Playwrights—modern plays and how they are made—Approximately one week

Actors—approximately one week

Directors—approximately one week

Designers: settings—approximately one week

Costumes—approximately one week

Lights–approximately one week

Makeup and sound—approximately one week

  ❶ ❷ ❸ ❹ ❺ ❻ ❼ ❽

➤ **Audiences and critics–one week**

The role of the audience; valuing the performance or production.

  ❺ ❻ ❼ ❽

➤ **Making theatre–six weeks (or more)**

Students will design and perform in short plays.

  ❶ ❷ ❸ ❹ ❺ ❻ ❼ ❽

Figure 2–1   There is nothing especially difficult about developing a course plan. The time-consuming and perhaps troubling aspect of course planning is making decisions about what will and what will not be taught. The course plan above calls for sixteen weeks of planned instruction; since most semesters are eighteen weeks, there is available time set aside for inservice days, assemblies, testing, and other school activities that can shorten the number of teaching days. Whatever days remain, they will be added to the Making Theatre unit.

Figure 2–1 can now be expanded to include reading assignments drawn from the text the school district has adopted. The example course plan cites *Theatre: Art in Action*. Another popular textbook that many schools use, *The Stage and the School*, also has well-illustrated material on most of these topics. There are other valuable texts that districts have adopted. Chapter 8 contains alternative texts and resources for the theatre teacher. Many schools also have copies of playscripts that the teacher may select to enhance the course content.

After the reading assignments are added, the teacher may wish to develop some broad learner objectives for this semester-long course. In short, the course outlined in Figure 2–1 can be revised, more fully developed, and much more detail can be documented. Or, if the teacher believes this brief outline is an adequate guide, then she can move to the next step in course planning: developing units.

Unit Planning

A unit is one section of a course—one discrete topic, subject, or theme—for which planned and coherent sequences of learning activities are structured over an extended period of time. Units do not have to occupy the same amount of time. Some can be short and others may take up one or more months of the semester. If the unit plan is to be effective in guiding the teacher, it should contain at least six areas.

➤ **Learner Objectives** These are what the teacher believes the student should be able to do and/or know about the topic after the unit is taught. Each objective should begin with the phrase, "The student will be able to . . ."

➤ **A List of the Content Standards This Particular Unit Addresses** Pinpointing specific standards will help the teacher select appropriate activities and content areas. A serious perusal of the content and achievement standards may also lead the teacher to link the unit to several standards thereby broadening the scope of learning.

➤ **An Introduction and Conclusion to the Topic** How the teacher enters and exits the unit is a vital part of the planning process. The introduction should engross the students and motivate them to want to learn. The conclusion should summarize the unit and lead to the next topic.

➤ **A Content Plan upon Which Classroom Instruction Can Be Based** The heart of the unit plan, it should follow directly from the learner objectives. The content plan is the information or concepts to be learned. If the content plan is not inherently connected to learning objectives, then learning may be jeopardized.

➤ **A List of Instructional Materials That Will Be Needed to Facilitate Learning** A complete list of the materials both students and teacher will need to complete the unit will remind the teacher of the necessary supplies needed, especially if those materials must be ordered.

➤ **Assessment** All assessment instruments should follow directly from the learner objectives and the content plan. The assessment plan should measure the success of learning the goals identified under learner objectives.

An ideal unit plan should incorporate a variety of learning activities that are student-centered—that is, activities for students to *do* rather than the teacher to *tell*. These specific content activities are the heart of daily lesson plans. Study the unit plan that follows (Figure 2–2). It should provide a model for other unit plans you might be asked to devise.

Unit: Actor-Audience Relationships:
Approximately Five Class Meetings

Learner objectives: At the conclusion of this unit, students will be able to

> **describe** with words and freehand sketches the actor-audience relationship of an arena, thrust, and proscenium theatre
>
> **identify** in writing one theatre from the past or present that employs each of the above actor-audience relationships by naming the theatre, its general dates of operation, its country of origin, and an event that was performed there
>
> **explain** at least three advantages and three disadvantages for play production using each actor-audience relationship

Standards addressed: ❶ ❷ ❸ ❹ ❺ ❽

Introduction: Where we sit in relationship to the stage in any theatrical space—coliseum, stadium, circuses as well as playhouses—affects our response to the program being presented. Explore with students their experiences at a sports event, school assembly, movie, television program, or rock concert. Arrive at a definition of actor-audience relationships.

Content: 1. Explore actor-audience relationships inherent in arena, thrust, proscenium spaces.

2. Present arena, thrust, proscenium theatres in various eras of theatre history. Make connections to various periods of theatre history by comparing and contrasting the dominant theatre configurations.

3. Discover which important plays have been written for particular actor-audience spaces.

4. Examine contemporary architecture in order to identify the actor-audience relationships. Have students seen these spaces in movies and television?

Instructional Materials: Models of theatres, magazine photos (Paris Opera House), videos capturing huge auditoriums (Crystal Cathedral), tour of school theatre (or other theatre spaces), copies of appropriate plays, clips from films that show various configurations such as *The Phantom of the Opera*. Board and markers. Student journals. Photographs of arena examples (Colosseum, basketball arena, circus). Cite pictures of proscenium, thrust, and arena in textbook.

Conclusion: Students will form five-member teams and will improvise a short scene and then stage it in each of the three actor-audience relationships. Discussion: What seem to be advantages/disadvantages of each relationship?

Assessment: Students will complete a journal entry on three advantages and three disadvantages of arena, proscenium, and thrust staging. In a short test, the students will draw freehand and label the parts of each configuration. On the same drawing, they will cite an import arena, thrust, and proscenium theatre, give its general dates, and name one play that was first produced there. (For example: a student might write: "Thrust: Globe, end of sixteenth century (beginning of seventeenth century) in London, England. Shakespeare's *Romeo and Juliet* was first performed there.") Students will demonstrate general understanding of the actor-audience relationships in proscenium, arena, and thrust configurations through participation in ensemble activities.

Figure 2–2 This unit plan is based on the course outline found in Figure 2–1. Does it meet the criteria for a unit plan that was described earlier?

Daily Lesson Planning

From unit plans, the teacher next constructs daily plans that set forth the specific content and the learning activities. A daily lesson plan, much like the unit plan, usually contains six parts: learner objectives, content and standards addressed, learning activities, materials of instruction, assessment, and new assignment. Its purpose is to help the teacher facilitate planning for the short term. The hallmark of an effective lesson plan is *specificity*; if the lesson plan is as generalized as the unit plan, for instance, then the lesson plan is ineffective as an instrument used in leading students to learn.

Schools may have a specific lesson plan format available for use, one that incorporates the particular layout and language that the school district prefers. Of course, the teacher should use the model endorsed by the district and/or the school. The daily lesson plan outline found in Figure 2–3, is but one of many generally accepted formats found in educational resources.

Daily Lesson Plan

Topic _____ Unit_____ Date _____

Learner objectives

_____

Content and standards addressed

_____

Learning activities

_____

Instructional materials

_____

Assessment

_____

New assignment

_____

Figure 2–3 Although this lesson plan format may look daunting, it can be completed by using key phrases. Once a plan is completed and the lesson taught, the plan should be revised by noting what the teacher discovered when teaching, and then saved for reuse.

The questions that follow will help to determine if the lesson plan is an effective teaching plan. These questions, in short, try to measure how specific the daily lesson plan is.

> ➤ **Are the learner objectives clear?** Do they relate to one or more theatre content standards? Are the descriptors clear? To which

of the achievement standards do the objectives relate? Can the learner objectives be easily assessed?

➤ **Are they significant?** Are the objectives focused? Or fuzzy? Or important?

➤ **Can the learner objectives be taught in the time allocated?**

➤ **Does the assessment directly connect to the learner objectives?** That is, can the objectives be taught using the activities listed?

➤ **Do the learning activities relate clearly, directly, and cogently to** **the learner objectives?**

The overriding question then, is: Do all of the parts of the lesson plan flow directly from the learner objectives? Study the lesson below (Figure 2–4). It is drawn from the unit plan above on actor-audience relationships.

Daily Lesson Plan: Third Day of a Five-Day Unit
Theatre I: Introduction to Theatre—Fifty-Minute Period

Topic: Arena Theatre Spaces   Date _____
Unit: Actor-Audience Relationships

Learner objectives: Students should be able to **sketch** the basic arena A-O relationship and **label** the parts; **identify** contemporary arena spaces in this locality; **list** important arena spaces from other times.

Content and standards addressed ❹ ❺ ❻ ❼
Parts of an arena space: stage, audience, actor entrance-exit tunnels (vomitoria), backstage spaces; reinforce that the building itself is not theatre, but a place for theatre to happen. Began with the Greeks (Thespis) but widely used today: football, basketball, circus, some concerts.

Learning activities: Have seats arranged in a circle before students enter; step into center and chat with the classs turning to take in all spectators; discuss this a-o relationship; show models of arena, proscenium, and thrust theatres. Ask: How are they different/alike? Devote five to eight minutes to allow students to write in journals of their perceived advantages and disadvantages of arena staging. Share examples of contemporary arena configurations; discover if students have experienced these. Distribute an incomplete schematic of an arena space and ask students to complete the drawing and label its parts. Show a video clip of a circus or other arena venue in use.

Instructional materials: Journals, video clips, pictures of various arena spaces, photos of arena productions, specific pages in the text that identify arena staging.

Assessment: Collect drawings. Read journal at a later time.

New assignment: Students are to discover what important plays were first performed in an arena setting.

Figure 2–4 This plan contains the areas usually found in most daily lesson plans: objectives, content outline, learning activities, instructional materials needed, assessment, and new assignment.

Play Production Scheduling

Planning a play production is similar to planning a course, a unit, or a single lesson. The master calendar must be consulted, the play scheduled, and rehearsals arranged. There is one major difference, however. Play production activities often take place outside of the normal class day.

Most new teachers will have had a depth of experience with the play production process through participation in college, university, or community theatre productions. They will have acted, probably directed, stage-managed, run crews, built scenery and costumes, gathered props, hung lights, or participated in the dozens of other activities that are involved in play production. In short, they will know it takes a lot of work by many people and a lot of time. Play production is treated in detail in Chapters 6 and 7.

Planning with Parents

Some school districts require teachers to inform parents of their course plans. Whether or not the school or the district requires parental involvement, it's a good idea to let the parents know what's going on in your classroom. Many schools require teachers to post syllabi and other classroom materials on the school's website. The following form (Figure 2–5) is one way to alert both parents and students to the requirements of your course. If you wish to include other information, it can be added.

Study the basics of the form in Figure 2–5 and adapt it to your needs. It may appear much like a syllabus you might receive in a college course.

Name of High School
Name of District

Course: Theatre III	Credit	Course Grading Scale
Teacher: your name		A = 93–100
Phone: your contact numbers		B = 85–92
Date: list start of class		C = 77–84
		D = 70–76
		F = 50–69

Approval:

_____

Administrator's Signature   Department Chair's Signature

The textbook, *Introduction to Theatre and Drama*, is provided.

Course Topics
[Here the teacher lists the topics to be covered during the course, usually taken from the course outline.]

Course Requirements
Daily Materials: Three-ring binder, paper, pen or pencil, texts when announced. Appropriate dress for movement and floor exercises on announced acting lab days.

Personal Portfolio: Four scheduled assessments. See attached rubric.

Daily: Class notes, small- and large-group work, discussions, individual reading, writing, research, performance preparation, and performances.

Homework: Reading, writing, memorization assignments(three to four days per week during some weeks).

Unit Projects: Research investigations, oral presentations, acting examination, aesthetic evaluation exercises, model creation.

Grading Procedures

20%: Course portfolio

80%: [Here the teacher lists the items that make up this part of the grade and notes the weight they will carry. These topics might include "The reading and analysis of five full length plays; presentation of five to eight acting scenes; direction of at least one scene, and so on."]

Late Work: All assignments are expected to be complete and on time to be considered for an A. Late work will be accepted, but 4 points per school day may be deducted. Tests missed due to absences must be made up within one week of absence. [If your school has a late work policy, it should be cited here.]

Extra Credit: Short reports related to the unit of study, aesthetic evaluation, and play participation.

Final Grade: Calculated as the average of each grading period.

Student Success: Only those assignments left undone will be considered failures.

Parent Contact: In addition to interim reports, phone notification will result from three absences and/or tardies, and if a student's grade drops below a C at any time during the course.

Detach and return bottom portion to teacher. Keep top portion for reference.

I have received and read the requirements and procedures for Theatre III.

_____

Parent's Signature   Date   Student's Signature

Figure 2–5 This form is intended for both student and parent. Note that the course grading scale should match the one that your school or district uses.

Plan for Supervisors

Teachers, for many reasons, are almost universally expected to provide the administration or their area supervisor with weekly lesson plans. Your supervisor will establish the number of times during the semester you must submit your weekly plans and how many weeks of instruction each submission must include. Because each teacher is responsible for delivering the curriculum, lesson plans provide a way to demonstrate to the supervisor and the district that this goal is accomplished. The teacher must not think of lesson plans as busywork. Planning is an invaluable tool for developing, maintaining, and demonstrating the teacher's subject matter competency and organizational skills.

The chart found in Figure 2–6 is a reproduction of one of the most popular formats that schools use to record the teacher's plans. The pages are bound and a semester's or a year's course outline can be listed. Although it is called a "lesson plan," there is not really enough space to record a detailed daily lesson plan, especially of the kind described earlier in this chapter. Rather, the new teacher should think of it as a matrix to record units of instruction along with homework assignments, text readings, and reminders of instructional materials needed.

Plan for Substitutes

All teachers must sometime absent themselves from the classroom for personal or professional reasons. Sometimes the teacher becomes ill. In these instances, a current lesson plan allows course work to be continued by a substitute teacher should the need arise. Typically, however, school administrators ask the teacher to generate a detailed substitute folder that includes all the information necessary for the management of the classroom during the teacher's absence. This material should include, among other material, information on students with special needs and a copy of classroom procedures.

As part of this substitute folder, the teacher is usually required to develop a three-day emergency plan for each class. These plans should fall into a general subject matter category and should be manageable for a substitute who has little or no knowledge of theatre. In reality, most teacher absences can be planned and lessons designed that are specific to the learner objectives that are currently being covered.

Consider that there may be only one theatre teacher on the faculty. In fact, there are areas of the country in which certified arts teachers are at a minimum and may actually fall into the category of critical needs. Therefore, it is not likely that a substitute teacher will be trained in a specific subject area, although she may have experience in classroom management. The key to success is to have established clear classroom procedures that will allow the students to proceed as independently as possible, leaving the substitute free to more easily manage the class, record attendance, and execute the lesson plan.

			Lesson Plan			
Subject					**Teacher's Name**	
Week					**Homeroom**	
Beginning						

Period/Subject	Monday	Tuesday	Wednesday	Thursday	Friday

Figure 2–6   Clearly this document can't accommodate all of the plans that the teacher will need for one week. However, many school districts still use it. Schedule a meeting with your supervisor to discover in some detail what is to be actually included in this plan.

Plan to Manage Your Classroom

Planning a clear classroom management strategy well before students arrive can have a profound effect in evoking appropriate student behavior. Your strategy should include the way you will establish classroom routines and procedures, methods to engender mutual respect in the classroom, the promotion of safety, the management of noise and space, and the development of a creative classroom environment. Different strategies work well for different teachers. But the beginning teacher should plan to develop management strategies before they are needed. During your career as a theatre teacher, you will find what approaches are effective in *your* classroom.

Classroom Environment   Your classroom is an extension of who you are and what you represent to your students. What your classroom looks like, how it is arranged, and the displays that are in it all reflect your teaching style. How interesting is it to your students? Because your subject is theatre, including media and the related arts, your classroom can become a vibrant, welcoming learning space.

Make your space stimulating, neat, orderly, and informal. Variety is just as important in the way you outfit your classroom as it is in the assignments you devise, the learning approaches you embrace, and the lessons you prepare. Bulletin boards, display cases, and posters should be changed regularly. Your students live in the fast-paced MTV world that is echoed in movies they see, video games they play, as well as television programs they watch. That is, students are accustomed to visual stimulation. Although the teacher can't compete with MTV flash in this regard, the classroom can become visually impressive when exhibits change with some frequency. A classroom that says you care about their enviornment will send a positive message to your students.

Routines and Procedures   Establishing clear and dependable routines and procedures can provide valuable benefits for teachers and students. When young people know what to expect from their teacher and know what is expected of them, a productive learning environment can develop effectively. Something as seemingly straightforward as entering and exiting the classroom may become challenging to manage depending on the age and personality of student groups. You will want to think about how to approach creating routines in your classroom through questions such as:

> ➤ Will students have assigned seats? If so, how will seating be arranged?
> ➤ Will they have routine places to store personal supplies?
> ➤ Will there be a communal storage space for shared materials?
> ➤ How will each class begin?
> ➤ What does student preparation mean?

There is no one right or wrong answer to any of these questions. Rather, there are answers that work more effectively for some teachers than others. These questions will be addressed more specifically in Chapter 3. As you and your students move through the school year, ask yourself periodically: Do the routines in my classroom support student learning? Are there procedures I might consider establishing that would further enhance a positive learning environment?

Respect Students and teachers need to trust that there is mutual respect in the theatre classroom. Address the issue of respect in written form at the beginning of the year, identifying behavior expectations and consequences for students who do not adhere to expectations. For instance, how will you establish procedures for listening and speaking in class discussions? What expectations might you want to explore with students about how to respect the contributions of all class members, particularly during feedback or critique situations? Think carefully about what you feel is truly important, keep behavior expectations simple and clear, and enforce consequences with consistency. Some teachers opt to use written behavior contracts with certain students or with an entire class, depending on their particular approach. In any case, share your expectations with parents as well as students.

Whatever issues you choose to address, they must be stated in a positive manner. Avoid beginning a classroom procedure with a negative. So, rather than "Do not push, shove, or harm others," phrase the desired result in the positive: "Respect your classmates; be polite." When you discuss this admonition with the class, raise the issue of what respect and politeness mean. The students, more than likely, will bring out that pushing and shoving is neither polite behavior nor respectful of others.

Discover the schoolwide expectations for students. Ask for copies of any student and teacher handbooks that outline the school policies and procedures. Make sure that your own classroom guidelines are aligned with the schoolwide expectations of students. Let your students know that you endorse and will enforce the school's discipline code.

The most effective teachers find ways of handling management issues within their own classrooms. Of course, this suggestion is not meant to imply that teachers should not seek administrative support for major issues of discipline; there are instances in which teachers must seek administrative involvement. When possible, however, demonstrate your professional capability by handling classroom management issues yourself with confidence and equanimity.

Safety Student safety is a primary concern for teachers. When setting up classroom and theatre spaces, think about how the physical environment supports student safety. What boundaries will you want to communicate with young people that will be important for maintaining their physical safety? Become familiar with the location of first aid supplies. Ensure that these supplies are current and fully stocked. Know and be able to carry out the procedures for handling accidents in your school. Observe fire drills with seriousness and single-mindedness. Prepare your students for the efficient and silent evacuation of your building.

Safety issues also include work spaces and the way they are managed. If you keep your classroom neat and organized, you automatically instill in your students a respect for the work that is carried out in that space. The same is true of the theatre space you will use and probably share with others. Make sure the junk left over from your previous show—lumber, flats, platforms, and the like—is disposed of in a safe manner or returned to the storage area. Paint cans must be tightly closed, brushes washed and dried, and both should be stored in the appointed place. Make sure used nails and screws are collected and properly disposed of. In short, if you keep your work spaces organized and free of clutter, your students will learn an important life lesson. You will also help to keep them safe. And you will earn the respect of the custodial staff upon whom you may have to call to help you out of a jam.

Personal and Emotional Safety You must consider your students' personal and/or emotional safety as a priority. For instance, clear boundaries in regards to what content and language is acceptable in improvisation activities must be spelled out. Students need (and want) you to set boundaries; if these parameters are not established, you may find some students willing to test them, to see "how far" they can go in scenes, improvisations, and acting exercises.

Sometime it is important for the teacher to touch a student to indicate proper breathing, for example, or to try and improve posture. Touching can lead to an inflammatory situation, even if it is done with the best of intentions, faultless propriety, and in front of other students. To prevent an unpleasant situation, new theatre teachers might wish to incorporate a statement, such as the one found in Figure 2–7, in the course materials.

The Physical Nature of Rehearsing and Performing

The body is the actor's true instrument. It is through the body (including voice production) that an actor communicates the script—be it formal or informal—to an audience. Consequently, the nature of performance training will at times require physical touch between instructor and student and/or between student and student in order to clarify or demonstrate the body's processes as related to actor training.

If you or your parents have any special needs or concerns or are uncomfortable with the nature of this work, or have past physical injuries that may restrict or prevent your taking part in the work, please make an appointment with me for further discussion. If you are uncomfortable discussing this with me, please see one of our Guidance Counselors.

Figure 2–7   A notice such as this one may prevent misunderstandings in classroom activities or production rehearsals. Before it is distributed to parents, this form should be approved by a supervisor.

Noise and Space   Managing a classroom includes monitoring noise and the use of space. Teachers have varying comfort levels with the amount of noise or "mess" in their classrooms. Several factors can come into play in determining how much is too much noise or mess. Are students actively engaged in the lesson and physically safe? Does the level of noise or use of space impede some students' learning? Are there other classes being conducted in close proximity to the theatre classroom that may be distracted by a high noise level? Establishing signals for attention and adjusting noise level can be very helpful to theatre teachers, even with older students.

Behavior Contracts   You may discover that different approaches are necessary depending on a particular group's needs. One teacher who had never used behavior contracts in ten years of teaching found it helpful to employ this technique with one particularly challenging class. You may also find it advantageous to discuss behavior strategies with other teachers in your school and district.

Monitoring and Adjusting the Plan

All planning is a work in progress. The teacher must always be prepared to monitor and adjust plans as needed. Accurately projecting the length of time a particular unit or lesson will take, for example, is something that occurs more easily after a teacher has had several experiences teaching a particular course.

Experienced teachers know that there is no perfect lesson plan or course outline. They know that what works once may not work the same way again, or vice versa. New teachers, however, must be mindful to make notes on all planning documents, from the course outline to the specific daily lesson plan, for future revision, reference, and reuse. Archive your documents for future use! Reinventing the wheel each year is not necessary, but building upon the previous year's successes is mandatory. Annotating lesson plans during and immediately after their completion is strongly recommended. It's also easy to do if the plans are archived on a reliable computer.

While at any point in the teaching process an idea may spontaneously arrive and prove itself to be extremely useful, it is building on the previous year's plan that will enable new teachers to grow and prosper in their schools. This practice will also ensure that the second year of teaching will be even more successful than the first year was.

EXTENSION ACTIVITIES

1. Construct a semester's course in acting using the planning model in this chapter. Duplicate the outline and share it with the class.

2. Based on the course plan developed in the previous activity, develop a unit plan for the acting course. Duplicate the plan and share it with the class.

3. Using the information from this chapter and your own ideas, plan a week's worth of developed lesson plans on any subject you wish. Duplicate your lessons to share with the class.

STAY CONNECTED

Bloom's taxonomy can provide you with dozens of learning outcome descriptors. A useful site can be found at www.coun.uvic.ca/learn/program/hndouts/bloom.html. You might also enter *Bloom's taxonomy* in a search engine to discover more details about Benjamin Bloom's fascinating work.

This site may help you locate theatre lesson plans: www.lessonplanspage.com/.

HELPFUL HINTS

➤ **Meet the Media People**   Get to know your media center personnel. Browse the library stacks and media support materials to find out what is already available to you. Learn the procedure for checking out these materials. Find out when and how they order books and materials and request that items you need are included. Be prepared to supply them with all the ordering information. It is also possible that your media center is equipped to tape timely items from the public education station for you to use in your classroom. They will know the copyright rules and time limits.

➤ **Use the Library**   Visit your local library to find out what is available for checkout and research. Most libraries have extensive collections of CDs, DVDs, and VHS tapes. Use this resource.

➤ **No Busywork**   Avoid giving assignments you are not willing to assess. Students resent anything that smacks of busywork.

➤ **Tame the Paper**   Deal with your "mail" first. It is very easy for the beginning teacher to become confused and overloaded with paperwork that seems unrelated to the classroom. Regardless, immediate attention should be given to the district and in-house mail you receive daily. Peruse it before your first class. Have a specific place for it on or near your workspace. Spend the first part of your planning period attending to it before moving on to other things. Avoid losing the ASAP item in the paper shuffle.

3

The Teacher in the Classroom
Getting Started

The teacher's activities in the classroom have often been likened to a performance. To the individual facing a roomful of captive individuals, some eager to hang on every word with others self-absorbed, it may seem impossible to tap dance fast enough to make it to the end of the hour, the day, the semester, the year. Certainly each teacher's personal style and energy affect how successful she will be in the classroom but she has more at her disposal. There are an array of well-understood approaches to teaching, with some methods focused on the teacher as star and others on the teacher as impresario who organizes the students in improvising their own teaching "performance." In addition, the teacher can manipulate the way the classroom is arranged, the procedures that are instituted in that classroom, and the expectations she establishes and enforces to keep the course on pace and the students engaged. The manner in which the teacher deals with issues of discipline, diversity, and gender also affects the teacher's ability to succeed in the classroom and in the school production program.

Teaching Methods and Learning Activities

Instructional methods, also called *teaching methods*, are the systematic techniques a teacher uses to help students learn. Instructional methods include, among others, lecture, demonstration, role-playing, and discussion. Teachers select appropriate methods that are designed to help students reach course, unit, or individual lesson goals.

It is vital for beginning teachers to discover how their particular students learn best. That is, different learning styles require different teaching methods and strategies.

Students may be

> ➤ **Auditory Learners**   They learn best by hearing someone talk to them or by listening to recordings.
> ➤ **Visual Learners**   They learn best by seeing: reading text material or what is on the board.
> ➤ **Tactile Learners**   They learn best by writing and touching objects.
> ➤ **Kinesthetic Learners**   They learn best through movement.

Most students learn by incorporating more than one learning style; no one teaching method is always the best choice for all students. Each student is different, and each student must be accommodated.

The most successful teachers use a wide variety of methods and creative strategies to enhance the learning environment. The highly skilled teacher learns to move subtly from one method to another, applying various strategies, and engaging in a variety of learning styles with no apparent break in the flow. Such ability stems from experimentation, effort, and experience. A theatre course has innate aspects that allow the imaginative teacher to meet student needs in numerous ways, to provide a wide variety of learning experiences, and to help students take ownership of their learning in a positive, creative environment.

The size of the class, the length of the class period, and the types of learners that are represented will influence choices the teacher makes about teaching methods and learning activities. For instance, a large class can limit the chances for individualized instruction or guidance by the teacher, while also affording a wider source of opportunities for student participation. The smaller class may be easier to manage, but can be limited in the opportunities for the exchange of ideas. When considering the length of the class period, some teachers may find that certain student-centered approaches can take more time to implement than is always available.

Definitions   Several key terms are used in this discussion that we define rather specifically. Consider the following four terms.

> ➤ *Instructional method* is a way of teaching used to accomplish a particular goal. Instructional methods may be teacher-centered or student-centered.
> ➤ *Learning activities* are the classroom activities developed from particular instructional methods.

> *Teacher-centered methodology* keeps the teacher in the leadership position, from which he sets the objectives and directs the learning process.

> *Student-centered methodology* encourages the student to be involved in the decision making for setting goals and to discover the significance of what is to be learned through a process of exploration and application.

Two Basic Questions   Although there are times when teacher-centered methods enhance student achievement of learning objectives, student-centered methods are very effective in enhancing student engagement and ownership. For each method, the significant questions are:

> What does the *teacher* do?
> What does the *student* do?

By considering these questions with care, the beginning teacher can contemplate which instructional methods might work effectively for various learning objectives. In addition, several particular strategies are outlined in this discussion to provide examples of learning activities.

Teacher-Centered Methods

Common teacher-centered methods include direct teaching, lecture, demonstration, and teacher-led discussion, as detailed in Figure 3-1. Beginning teachers will want to consider how these methods can be used effectively in their classrooms.

Teacher-Centered Method	What Does the Teacher Do?	What Does the Student Do?	Some Applications of This Method
Direct teaching	Provides prompts that require specific responses (rote memory and recall)	Offers response to teacher prompt (individually, in groups, or as an entire class)	Introduction or review of lesson or unit; practice; games; peer tutoring
Lecture	Delivers information	Listens, takes notes, completes other assignments generated from the lecture	Lecture outline; graphic organizers; time lines; audio and visual aids; variation: minilecture

Teacher-Centered Method	What Does the Teacher Do?	What Does the Student Do?	Some Applications of This Method
Demonstration	Shows or exemplifies a process or procedure	Observes, may take notes, or applies a process or procedure to assignment	Guided practice; model creation; physical expression
Teacher-led discussion	Asks questions related to or building upon information previously delivered	Responds to teacher questions and to other student responses	Development of cultural and historical contexts; synthesis of information; response to theatre and other media

Figure 3–1 Each of the four methods cited put the teacher at the center of the learning and the student on the periphery. As you study this chart, give some thought to how the application of each method might appear in the theatre classroom.

In today's classroom, the teacher may have access to computers, programs such as PowerPoint, computer projectors, and many other tools, depending on the particular school and district. Go beyond the overhead projector; your students have! Explore your school's technology possibilities to maximize student success with all teacher-centered methods.

Direct Teaching This method, sometimes called *recitation*, is a quick question-and-answer format. The teacher asks, the student answers. The teacher is a fact checker, if you will, perhaps asking students to "Name three important Greek playwrights of tragedy" or "When did the Globe burn to the ground?" Direct teaching is an excellent method to review a unit by summarizing salient facts. Much factual material can be covered in a short period of time.

Student involvement in direct teaching can be increased by dividing the class into academic teams to determine which team can answer correctly the most questions. There will be even more student involvement if the teacher asks each student to contribute three short-answer questions based on a unit, thus providing the questions for direct teaching. Because direct teaching emphasizes recall and memory (for example, dates or lines for a play), teachers will want to employ other methods to discover if the student understands the significance of the facts.

Lecture This method requires the teacher to make an organized presentation that is clear, informative, interesting, and cogent. Clearly, the teacher does the presenting while students listen. The lecture is an efficient and appropriate way to introduce or summarize a unit of study, to furnish background information, or to focus student activities. Although some teachers use the lecture method almost exclusively, it is best to combine lectures with one or two student-centered methods. There are multiple variations to the lecture method that can enhance student learning. Remember the old adage, "*Telling* is not *teaching*." Some ways to adapt the lecture method include the minilecture, note-taking strategies, and the use of technology.

The minilecture involves dividing a lecture into short segments, interspersed with audiovisual experiences or opportunities for active student engagement. Perhaps a minilecture might cover the nature of poetic verse as it appears in a play by one of the great tragic playwrights of ancient Greece. Interspersed with the presentation of the facts, a short scene from a production of a Greek play might be shown, the same or another scene read aloud, or a short scene from an opera that includes recitative and part of an aria might be played or shown.

Taking effective notes can be a demanding enterprise for many students. Some students are challenged by listening, writing, and recognizing key points at the same time. Teachers can employ various strategies to note taking that help students collect and maintain the information necessary to be successful. Consider the potential value of the following suggestions.

➤ encouraging students to tape-record lecture material

➤ allowing students to use laptop computers

➤ structuring student pairs to take turns taking notes

➤ allowing students who take notes well and enjoy taking notes to become scribes for those who encounter challenges

➤ using a teacher-prepared lecture skeleton outline that allows the students to listen more and fill in definitions and facts as they come up during the information delivery

➤ placing modified lecture material online on the school's website

Whatever options are available in your classroom, consider how you can use opportunities beyond the chalk or marker board to support student learning through teacher-centered methods. Provide students, for example, with a partial outline of a lecture to be filled in as needed. Through this approach, which can be useful for a wide variety of activities including time lines, charts, plot structure, character analysis, and much more, the teacher may continue to make eye contact with students with a modified version of the student outline appearing on the overhead, projector screen, or television screen.

Demonstration Also called *modeling,* this method requires a teacher or another expert to show how something is done. For example, the teacher might demonstrate the correct way to shadow and highlight a face as part of the technique for old age makeup. Or, the teacher could model certain acting techniques such as beginning and ending a stage cross with the upstage foot extended. Another example might include disassembling an ellipsoidal lighting instrument to reveal its double lens system and comparing that lens system with the Fresnel, a single step-lens instrument. In all demonstration teaching, the presenter is the expert and the students observe, take notes, and (perhaps) ask questions.

Teacher-Led Discussions Of the four teacher-centered methods listed here, teacher-led discussions involve students the most. This method asks the teacher to pose exploratory questions for which there are no definitive answers. That is, this method is far from the direct teaching method in which questions are asked that have uncontested answers.

Appropriate questions for teacher-led discussion might include the following: Why are there so few women's roles in Shakespeare's plays? Are the plays of Sophocles (*Oedipus Rex*) more enjoyable than the plays of Euripides (*Medea*)? Why? How strong was the production we saw yesterday at the community theatre? Can you separate the merits of the play from the merits of the production? In short, these kinds of questions require student understanding and synthesis of materials and concepts rather than rehearsal of the known.

Teacher-led discussions should have strong introductions and conclusions. For example, a film clip from *Shakespeare in Love* might precede the discussion of the role of women in Shakespeare's theatre. A mock debate format might be introduced by the teacher to add zest to the discussion. Those students favoring *Oedipus Rex* might sit on one side of the room and those favoring *Medea* on the other.

The discussion should always be concluded, not just stop. Using the sample question about separating the playscript from the production, the teacher should conclude the discussion by redacting the differences between what was in the script and what was (or was not apparent) in the production. Students should be called upon to help synthesize the discussion.

Student-Centered Methods

There are multiple methods that place students at the center of their learning experiences. Several commonly used methods include student-led discussion, cooperative learning, role-playing, and inquiry/discovery. While examining Figure 3–2, think about the potential benefits and possible drawbacks of the student-centered methods described. For instance, small- and large-group student-led discussions can provide valuable opportunities for students to learn *with* and *from* one another, to share experiences, and to take ownership of knowledge they gain through working with peers. Some young people, however, may find it challenging to engage productively in such discussions, perhaps from a personal lack of confidence or the fear of wasting time.

Student-Centered Method	What Does the Teacher Do?	What Does the Student Do?	Some Applications of This Method
Student-led discussion/ seminar groups	Prepares structure for students to lead discussion; recaps or fills in gaps	Plans and leads discussion, builds thinking and interpersonal skills	Reading and research; large- and small-group projects.
Cooperative learning	Implements structure for student work in pairs and groups	Collaborates with other students to accomplish specified learning outcome	Group problem solving; study for tests or presentations; group creation of informal or formal theatre
Role-playing and games	Designs procedure that asks students to engage in role	Explores feelings, behavior, problems, consequences and related factors through taking on a role	Living histories; biographical inquiry; character analysis
Inquiry/Discovery	Provides information and/or access to information; aids in shaping the direction of the inquiry/discovery	Develops knowledge and skills by independent research focused on solving a problem	Independent research; emphasis on research process; gathering data; communicating information

Figure 3-2 What content standards and learning objectives do you think would work well with each of these student-centered methods? How might teacher preparation time and use of class time be affected by each method?

Clearly the teacher is the principal focus of the classroom in teacher-centered methods and student-centered methods place much classroom leadership into the hands of her students. This very fact may mean that efficiency is sacrificed for student involvement and ownership.

Student-Led Discussion   When students are discussion leaders, the teacher is responsible for preparing the student discussion leader in advance of the scheduled discussion. Consideration should be given to the structure of the questions and the form the discussion will take. Questions similar to those previously cited as appropriate topics for teacher-led discussions are models for the framework of student-led discussion.

These discussions, however, can take many forms, including *panel discussion* in which a question is established and panel members who, because of their prior research, each present a facet of the topic as an expert. The discussion leader introduces the presenters, and after the preselected panel members have spoken, the audience of other students in the class is asked to participate in the discussion by questioning the presenters, adding their opinions, or commenting on what was presented. Disagreement is welcomed. The student leader becomes a moderator.

The student-led discussion may take the form of a two-person debate, for example, where two preselected students speak, one in favor of the question for discussion and the other opposed. There may be a panel of predetermined "experts" who then have several minutes to question the two speakers. Then the moderator opens the discussion to the entire class.

No matter what the form, the student discussion leader ensures that participation is distributed throughout the class. The leader should also be well versed in the topic so, if discussion falters, he can ask the audience questions that will ensure the discussion does not die on its feet.

As students develop skill with the interpretation of their research, the teacher might like to explore more fully the panel discussion approach in which students become responsible for researching and presenting teachable items to the rest of the class. Ultimately, the entire class is expected to participate in a culminating activity or assessment, so each team is equally responsible for their research and their seminar presentations. For example, students might explore the development of theatre in Spain, France, and England during the late Renaissance or Neoclassical periods or perhaps a unit on the development of the American musical.

Cooperative Learning   Another example of student-centered teaching is cooperative learning, in which students work collaboratively in pairs or groups to complete an activity or assignment. This method provides students the opportunity to share and learn the value of joint effort. At the same time it can be challenging for the teacher to monitor student progress of multiple groups working simultaneously.

Cooperative learning is most effective when the student grouping is structured to include students of different strengths and learning styles. This strategy will encourage productive cooperation. Team members will learn from each other. Consider the pros and cons of giving group grades versus individual grades.

The teacher may choose, for instance, to supply the class with a list of theatrical styles (realism, expressionism, symbolism, naturalism, and so on). The class is divided into groups, as suggested above, so that each group has a theatrical style to explore. The groups are then directed to specific online websites or hard-copy text resources. Each team is then scheduled to present to the class a description of the style and its significance. Each team plans to teach their section in any way they wish (musical selections, posters, game show format, crossword puzzles, selected passages from representative scripts, time lines, and so on) as long as the significance of each theatrical style is clearly established. With the teacher serving as resource, guide, and moderator, this cooperative learning approach can be very effective as it increases student-centered learning opportunities.

In a partner or small-group setting, students may benefit from the direction that outline diagrams can give to collaborative interpretation of information. The outline diagram is a document written by a group for distribution to the class. For instance, in a unit on improvisation, the teacher might assign different sections of the textbook's chapter on improvisation to different groups. Each team would review, discuss, and divide the labor for its group's synthesis outline on their section of the chapter. Teams might also plan to lead the class in appropriate improvisation exercises that best exhibit the important points selected for their outline. Copies of the team's document would be distributed during the members' presentation on their section of the improvisation chapter; this shared student-centered outline of knowledge could be the basis for various kinds of assessment.

Role-Playing and Games   Theatre students usually enjoy theatre games and improvisations. The teacher should be selective with these activities and guide the students through question-and-answer and personal/peer feedback opportunities. Theatre games should have a purpose and need to be planned accordingly. For example, helping students to develop concentration skills, listening skills, trust, or the like can be achieved with various games and improvisation activities.

Inquiry/Discovery   These two teaching methods, inquiry and discovery, are closely related but not quite identical. Both methods are, in essence, guided independent research. Discovery uses research to gather evidence (data), document it, analyze it, and evaluate its importance. Inquiry is closely allied to discovery but is focused on problem solving using the five-step scientific method:

> ➤ identification of a problem
> ➤ listing of possible solutions
> ➤ gathering of data
> ➤ analysis and interpretation of data
> ➤ testing of solutions until one is identified

The student is thus required to develop assumptions, draw inferences, think logically, and apply information in order to solve a problem.

In both these processes the teacher is a guide. She might identify sources of information or help the student phrase the specific research questions. Her day-to-day involvement will depend on the student, that is, varying according to how much supervision and guidance the student requires to facilitate learning. Does the student need careful maintenance? Periodic monitoring? Hardly any oversight? There are compelling issues in theatre that will benefit from such an approach. For example, a student might develop a daybook for a local community theatre covering one or two years, be they calendar years or production years. This means the investigator would examine the theatre's records to determine how each day was spent ❺.

> ➤ What takes place in this theatre on a day-by-day basis?
> ➤ What days were devoted to set building and rehearsals?
> ➤ What days were devoted to performance?
> ➤ What plays were performed?

Once the data is collected, conclusions can be drawn, depending, of course, on the original question. The question might be any one (or a combination) of the following.

> ➤ How can this theatre space be used more efficiently?
> ➤ What kinds of plays are usually produced?
> ➤ What kind of plays are most successful with audiences?
> ➤ How many days does a typical production in this theatre rehearse?

> ➤ Could the theatre produce more plays if the scenery was built in a difference space?

Four Sample Learning Activities

The different teaching methods discussed previously can be developed into specific classroom learning activities. Study the four activities that follow. Note the teaching methods that are used. As you consider the examples provided here, keep in mind that there are a vast number of different activities that can be useful in theatre study. As you discover new learning activities during your career, create a filing system that you maintain and update regularly.

The examples that follow use different learning methods to craft strategies particular to a theatre classroom. As you consider these examples, think about how you might develop one or more of the methods described earlier to articulate specific theatre-related strategies. As mentioned previously in this book, the standards identified in connection with particular activities *may* be addressed, depending on how the individual teacher approaches the material.

Living Journal with Still Images and Captions ❶ ❷ ❸ ❹ ❺ ❻ ❼ ❽

This sample activity employs the student-centered methods of inquiry or discovery and cooperative learning. It seems appropriate for high school students and may take a week to complete as research must be conducted and analyzed. Students are engaged in small groups. Each team chooses an influential actor or director from a specified period, such as the first half of the twentieth century in American theatre or film. Essential questions include: What is important about this actor or director? What contribution(s) did this person make to the field of theatre or film? Once students have identified their subject and gathered information to answer the essential questions, the following strategies are required by group members.

> ➤ Identify three important moments of the actor or director's career. In deciding which moments to include, consider: If this person wrote a journal about their life and career, which three achievements or experiences would this actor or director consider especially significant?
>
> ➤ Create three different still images that embody the three important moments described above. Make sure to incorporate all members of the group. (Still images, also called *tableaux,* can

be described as a moment frozen in time, as if you are representing a photograph that was taken at a particular instant.)

➤ Decide upon three different captions of one or two sentences to accompany the three still images. Write each caption on a separate index card and put the cards in chronological order according to the historical figure's life events. These captions might be taken from the figure's own words or text written about the person; the group may also invent original captions.

➤ Present a living journal of the historical figure to the rest of the class. A classmate who is not a group member can be asked to read each of the captions in succession. As each caption is stated, group members will create the still image for that moment from the actor or director's life.

➤ After all groups' living journals have been shared with the class, the class may engage in reflective discussion and brainstorming. What have students discovered about actors and directors during the specified period? What similarities and differences did they notice in the images and captions?

The Character Trace ❸ ❺ ❻

The following activity builds particularly on the student-centered method of cooperative learning. This approach provides students with multiple ways of understanding and analyzing a character within one group activity. This version of the character trace seems especially appropriate for grades eight and nine; if a different, simpler text were used, this strategy would be appropriate for grades six and seven.

Some students may benefit especially from approaching a character physically. Others prefer understanding how the given circumstances affect the character they are exploring. The character trace works well when an entire class is familiar with the same play. The sample activity described here assumes that the students have read and studied a translation of Euripides' *Medea*. Strategies might include the following activities.

After reading Euripides' *Medea*, each academic team will meet and choose a character from the play.

➤ Each team chooses a different character. The character choice is approved by the teacher to avoid duplication before proceeding any further.

➤ A member of the team lies down on a sufficient length of butcher paper as another team member traces her outline onto the paper.

➤ Using the markers, colored pencils, and other materials provided, team members work together to complete the character trace as described below.

➤ Complete the trace by designing an appropriate costume and supplying features for the character.

➤ Write the name of the character at the top of the trace.

➤ Find a quotation in the script in which the character expresses something about himself. Write that quotation above the trace.

➤ Find a quotation in the script in which another character expresses something about the character on the trace. Write that quotation below the trace.

➤ Choose five adjectives that describe the character. Write the adjectives anywhere on the trace.

➤ Present the trace to the class by the end of the class period.

Ground Plan Development ❸ ❹ ❺ ❻ ❼

This strategy builds on the method of demonstration, followed by guided practice wherein students apply the process that has been modeled. This ground plan project is particularly suited to high school students and should occupy about a week.

At the beginning of the lesson, the teacher shows students a sample of a ground plan that has been designed for their school's theatre space, preferably a plan for a set that students have previously worked with. The teacher demonstrates how to establish scale for a ground plan and how to make choices about placement of doors, furniture, platforms, flats, and other items. The materials used for this demonstration could be as simple as a drawing on the board or projector; a PowerPoint presentation could also be an effective choice for the demonstration. The resourceful teacher might consider adapting the felt boards often seen in early childhood settings for this activity.

Following the demonstration, students engage in guided practice as they create their own ground plans for assigned plays. Steps for the guided practice activity are described as follows:

➤ Create in scale size the various objects needed for the ground plan. Use the colored construction paper and scissors provided to craft scale representations of furniture, doors, platforms, and other items as needed.

➤ On the graph paper provided, outline the performance area in the same scale as the objects created in step one.

➤ Arrange items for the ground plan on the graph paper performance area, making sure to consider the requirements of the ground plan checklist.

➤ When satisfied with the arrangement of the ground plan, affix the items to the graph paper using the adhesive provided. Make sure not to use permanent glue, as the placement of the set pieces on the ground plan may change.

➤ After students have practiced creating individual ground plans, they may share their work with the class. Based on feedback from the teacher and other students, each student may opt to change placement of set pieces on the graph paper as desired.

Theatre Production

Because productions for public performance are often prepared outside school hours, it is likely that some students' schedules will not allow for their full participation. Some students, too, though they participate in acting activities in class as part of the curriculum, would prefer to develop the backstage skills all productions require. Rather than simply expose the students to the definitions and lists of responsibilities of management and running crew positions or how-to descriptions of set, costume, makeup, lighting, and sound fabrication and application, the teacher is encouraged to find ways to allow the students to discover the need for these aspects of theatre during class as much as possible.

This first classroom activity is built on the method of cooperative learning and inquiry or discovery ❷ ❸ ❹ ❺ ❻ ❼ ❽. The teacher selects an even number of appropriate ten-minute plays. The selection should ensure that each student is cast. As students prepare for these performances, which may be for the most part self-directed, the teacher might wish to pair scenes in such a way that one set of actors provides technical support for another and vice versa. The cast of play one, for example, will design and produce play two. The cast of play two will produce and design play one. This pairing will allow students to recognize the importance of all aspects of the theatrical whole within classroom endeavors.

This second classroom activity is also based on the methods of cooperative learning and inquiry or discovery ❸ ❺ ❻ ❼ ❽. After several public performances of two or three plays have been given, the teacher encourages older or more experienced students to develop a technical manual that applies what they have learned about producing plays in the school's space. This manual should reflect what the students feel are the best ways to present a successful production in the particular school's facilities. In this way, a tradition can be initiated, while the practical requirements taught in the classroom are clearly learned and implemented for production work. Sections of the manual might include

➤ managing the lighting, including an inventory of lighting instruments and cable

➤ managing the property storage areas, including an inventory of set props like furniture, carpets, lamps, and the like

➤ managing the scenic elements, including an inventory of flats and platforming by size

If possible, the teacher should provide opportunities for the students to actually research and build their own sets and costumes. However, this may prove difficult if space and budgetary restrictions do not permit.

Taking students to see theatre is extremely important as they learn to interpret theatre and respond to what they see. The teacher may find that many students have rarely attended a live production of a play. The experience of responding to a theatrical performance can provide students with the key to understanding how the textbook, their classroom experiences, and their public performances are all related. Learning to evaluate the work of others better helps the student learn to evaluate her own work. The teacher also benefits from this shared experience with students.

Some Teaching Strategies

Teaching strategies, as used here, are universally useful techniques, no matter the subject or method used in teaching. For the experienced teacher, teaching strategies are well-entrenched habits of mind and tools of communication. Here three strategies are offered. To build a strong integrated structure for your students to remember and identify different concepts, the teacher must organize material in multiple ways. To focus and deepen student exploration, students must be able to identify key words and essential questions. And to create and reinforce expectation, the teacher must regularly post goals in the classroom.

Organize Thematically as Well as Chronologically

Teacher-centered methods offer efficient ways to convey information about theatre from various times and cultures. However, the teacher may find that following the chronology of theatrical development from ancient Greece to modern times might be too time-consuming or that students find it difficult to recognize the need to return to the past when the theatre they do is actually a present-day activity in a modern theatrical venue. Working from a thematic approach involves movement back and forth in time and across cultures as students discover a wide range of theatre styles, innovations, and concepts. *Thematic organization* is arranging materials topically.

The broad concepts of tragedy or comedy, for instance, could be explored thematically by examining how these concepts are exhibited now, how they have changed over time, how they have stayed the same, and how they are interpreted in different cultures. Other topics, such as coming of age, parent-child relationships, social problems, and the like provide the teacher with a wide range of themes that address theatre standards in ways that will be relevant to young people.

Use Key Words and Phrases and Essential Questions

Additional approaches that may help shape student-centered methods include *operative words and phrases* and *essential questions.* Mutual exploration of operative words can include having a chart posted in a specific place in the classroom to which students and teacher may add basic terms, significant phrases, and names of important innovators. Reference to this list provides automatic opportunities for review or discussion, for journal writing, and for student discovery of the relationship between content and practice. If, for instance, a unit in theatre management is appropriate, then the teacher might post the essential words and phrases that follow at the beginning of the unit to introduce the unit. A carefully selected list of key words and phrases could provide the teaching outline for the unit ❸. Students could then add to the list or define the following terms: *front of house, scaling the house, box office report, audit, comps, earned income, stub,* and *producer.* Encouraging students to participate and take ownership of an operative word list will enhance their theatre vocabulary and broaden their understanding of the art form.

Establishing essential questions provides students with reasons an area of study is significant. Identifying a goal early on, giving students clues about what to look for, and posting questions that focus attention on the essence of the unit, lesson, or activity can prove to be very helpful for the students as well as the teacher.

Essential questions encourage students to synthesize knowledge and to design purposeful applications. For instance, essential questions posed during different theatre history units might include the following examples: Why are the performing arts ephemeral experiences? Was William Shakespeare a fluke or a logical product of his own time? What do the people of the Renaissance owe to the artists and scholars of the medieval period? Students can be invited to identify their own essential questions at the beginning, middle, or end of a lesson or unit. For example, students working together on a devised scene might pose one or more questions to guide their group process.

Consider the following essential questions that were posed by one eleventh-grade class that studied improvisation. What is the nature of improvisation? What is its purpose? What are the elements common to all successful improvisations? How can I plan and execute a successful improvisation with a partner and with a group? How does the improvisation influence the development of the open-ended scene? This example shows the depth and breadth of ideas that can arise from involving the class in formulating essential questions.

Post Weekly Goals

Students and teachers alike find it helpful to rely upon shared expectations of what each week's classroom experiences will entail. Post them for the mutual benefit of the students as well as the teacher. The beginning theatre teacher can benefit from developing a pattern of how different days of the week are used on a consistent basis. For example, the teacher might assign a performance activity on a Monday that is to be presented the following Friday. This pattern provides the student time outside of class to develop the performance according to the preestablished performance rubric. During the remaining class days that week, content-centered activities such as reading, research, rehearsal, and project development might take place. Student interest may be more easily maintained when a regular shift between what they should *know* about theatre and how they *do* theatre is used.

Classroom Procedures and Expectations

It's your classroom! The success of your instructional methods and learning activities are directly affected by the approach to classroom procedures and the established expectations. Establish reasonable but clear expectations and procedures that all students are asked to honor.

The teacher who develops a consistent set of classroom procedures, regardless of the specific instructional methods being used on any given day, can provide the structure and direction that students need. Consistency in a teacher's style implies neither a static nor an unimaginative approach. Rather, consistency is an important strength that can set a pattern of initiative that takes students to new levels of discovery and self-reliance.

As a beginning teacher, you are encouraged to consider what kinds of daily classroom procedures you feel will be important to establish in your new classroom. A posted list of procedures and expectations can be a helpful tool of classroom management. One middle school teacher phrased his classroom expectations as "theatre talk" with the teacher playing the role of director and the students cast as actors. See Figure 3–3.

Ten Suggestions for Success in Theatre *and* Life

1. **Entrances and exits** Actors will arrive promptly and work diligently during the session. Actors will not bring food or drink other than water into the rehearsal hall.

2. **Dressing room** Actors' personal property will be stowed in the appropriate location.

3. **Props and scenery** Actors will not touch anything in the rehearsal hall that doesn't belong to them without permission. Actors will return property to its original location.

4. **Asides** Actors are expected to have done whatever homework was assigned by the director by the time expected.

5. **Places** Actors will be silent, seated, and prepared for the first act on the bell cue.

6. **Blocking** Actors will stay in their seats unless directed to do otherwise.

7. **Stage combat** Actors will not argue or physically touch another actor unless directed to do so.

8. **Cues** Actors will give the director a cue that they want to talk during discussions by raising their hand.

9. **Audience** Actors will listen when another actor is talking.

10. **Show time** Actors will present all assignments by the assigned deadline. There are no understudies to do the actors' homework.

Curtain calls Break a leg, have fun, and learn about theatre!

Figure 3–3 These classroom expectations are phrased in a novel way using theatre jargon, yet the teacher's intent remains clear.

Experienced teachers almost always communicate classroom expectations either by posting them in the classroom or on their school's website. It's important for students (and parents!) to know what behaviors are anticipated by the teacher.

In addition to behavioral expectations, the teacher should devise daily procedures. Although these, too, have a behavioral expectation, the thrust of these daily classroom procedures is how a class is to begin (Figure 3–4).

Daily Procedures

➤ Get settled and ready to work.

➤ Check the board for the day's activities and essential question.

➤ Place any assignments due in the assignment box.

➤ Pick up all graded work and file accordingly.

➤ Proceed with starter activity.

➤ Be prepared to begin the day's assignment at the scheduled time.

Figure 3–4 How is this list similar to or different from procedures you experienced as a student yourself? What might the list of procedures look like in a classroom where you are the theatre teacher?

While the students move through the daily initiating procedures, the teacher may simultaneously take roll and deal with any required administrative procedures with a minimum loss of class time. Following this type of pattern consistently will help the students learn quickly what is expected. It will also allow the teacher some time to shift gears more smoothly as classes change during the day.

Figure 3–4 assumes that the teacher has established a place for students to leave assignments that need to be assessed, a place from which students may retrieve graded assignments, and a process for saving or maintaining completed work. With some schools emphasizing portfolio development or exhibition of mastery at the end of a course or school year, the teacher is advised to develop some sort of student filing system for work that should be kept. This will prove very helpful for the student who chooses to follow the theatre program offerings over a period of several semesters. In addition, Figure 3–4 mentions a *starter activity*, which offers students a structured opportunity to be productive as soon as they are settled in the classroom.

Starter Activity   This activity is especially designed to engage students the moment they enter the classroom. Starter activities are intended to be completed in the first five to eight minutes of class while the teacher attends to administrative matters. Well-designed starter activities keep students on track no matter when they enter the classroom.

Starter activities can take many forms. Here are some to consider. Students can

- ➤ run lines for a performance assignment
- ➤ write journal entries prompted by quotations exhibited on a board or screen
- ➤ respond in their journals to timely articles on a relevant aspect of theatre
- ➤ evaluate in writing one or two peer performances, or evaluate their own performance
- ➤ respond in their journal to one of the posted essential questions that accompanies the unit
- ➤ study a particular set of illustrations (not previously assigned) found in the textbook
- ➤ read a short play

These examples illustrate the nature of starter activities. Note, too, that the starter activity can also provide valuable in-class reading time for students. Encouraging theatre students to read very short plays you have collected that represent different theatrical styles and cultures is a very rewarding guided activity that will not only expand their general knowledge of drama but will allow them the opportunity to discover the similarities and differences within genres and gain a clearer understanding of how plays work.

Classroom Management

The classroom procedures and established expectations all affect the way you manage your classroom. The previous chapter asked you to *plan* for effective classroom management by presenting theoretical questions for reflection. This discussion is devoted to the *practical ways* in which a classroom can be effectively managed. The goal, of course, is to lay the groundwork for a classroom environment that will allow cogent and efficient learning. Such considerations as the arrangement of the classroom and the teacher's own behavior will help to ensure that the classroom is well managed. First, a well-managed classroom is an orderly classroom. Keep the space organized and neat. Students will more likely follow the teacher's example and pick up after themselves without the teacher having to prompt such action.

Consider the physical arrangement of the classroom, for example. Try to break the traditional arrangement of the teacher's desk in the front of the classroom with student desks arranged to face the teacher. Your desk may appear at the back or side of the classroom, for example, rather than at the front. Tables and chairs in various configurations instead of student desks may set your classroom apart from those of other teachers. Or, if the table and chair arrangement is not possible, the desks may be arranged in a variety of patterns that encourage discussion, allow for a smoother move into group work, and also provide more areas for presentations. Arrangements should also make it possible for you to move throughout the classroom with ease and support student learning in various parts of the space. Some theatre classrooms even have reading corners with comfortable furniture that may be used on occasion.

The teacher's persona is also a key to classroom management. The ideal teacher is

- ➤ consistent in her behavior
- ➤ firm in her requests for classroom order
- ➤ quick to address student misbehavior
- ➤ respectful herself and requires respect from her students

Most of all, the effective teacher does not threaten her students. This quality has two implications. First, her demeanor is open, encouraging, supportive, and, above all, not antagonistic. Second, the teacher does not make disciplinary assertions that can't be fulfilled.

With all these caveats, the new teacher can still be herself if she will only remember that her relationship with her students is not a personal one but a professional one. You may like your students but you are not their personal friend—you are their *teacher*. Thus getting angry at a student is a personal reaction, not a professional one. The teacher must be, first and foremost, a professional.

Diversity in Your Classroom

Curriculum plans and classroom teaching activities must consider diversity as traits like a student's race, class, and gender all affect learning. Diversity can include not only race, class, and gender but also economic status, religion, age, culture, ethnicity, sexual orientation, language, learning styles, physical ability, and educational background, among other factors. Diversity is not just good social policy; research has shown that celebrating diversity in the school can improve educational outcomes. Diversity programs are communitywide endeavors, beyond the control of an individual teacher. Still the theatre teacher has a special opportunity for influence beyond the classroom, to include the entire community, through the uses of diversity in the theatre production program.

When diversity is recognized and is celebrated, students become better learners. In recent years, numerous publications on theatre and education have urged strategies to celebrate diversity in the classroom. By seeking out resources, the beginning theatre teacher can draw on a wealth of educators' experiences to shape classroom activities that deliver positive messages about individual differences.

Young people will have more genuine experiences with exploring diversity through theatre arts when the work is student-focused and provides opportunities for young people to *do*, not just to listen and receive. Educators communicate with students about diversity by how they approach theatre in the classroom. The materials selected to support learning, for example, will surely communicate the teacher's sensitivity (or insensitivity) to issues of diversity. That is, the plays chosen for informal and formal performances, the subjects the teacher provides for improvisations and devising, and the degree to which the teacher is Eurocentric in selecting examples to support learning all reveal how aware the teacher is of the diversity within her classroom. Inclusive casting policies also demonstrate diversity issues. In your classroom can *any* student be considered for any role? Students are aware, also, of what school events teachers attend. If they only attend sports events played by male athletes, a message can be read that is clear and unambiguous. The same is true of campuswide cultural events.

Teachers and students alike must seek authentic information and construct meaningful experiences for their students. Don't make uninformed assumptions about cultures, such as assuming that a Latin American theatrical tradition would be the same as a tradition originating from Spain, Portugal, Mexico, Puerto Rico, or another geographical origin.

Statistically, teachers tend to be different from their student population. A University of Maryland study recently found that considering all teachers and students in K–12 classrooms, 75 percent of teachers are female and 84 percent of all teachers are white yet 40 percent of all public school students are composed of various minorities and the gender breakdown of the student body is about 50/50. A teacher cannot ignore the differences but must actively work to bridge gaps between herself and her students. The best way to do so is to encourage the students to "teach" each other and the teacher about their own perspectives—of race, culture, gender, and the like. Without an atmosphere of openness and civility, such discussions cannot take place and the diverse classroom will be less than fully realized.

Gender in Your Classroom

Although the broad category of diversity can be interpreted as including gender issues, it may be useful to think about gender specifically through questions such as:

➤ How do educational choices value and respect all people?

➤ What do young people perceive it means to be a man or a woman in society today?

➤ What factors do adolescents understand as contributing to gender roles? (Possibilities include family relationships, romance, careers, emotions, and educational choices among many other dynamics that can affect how young people define gender roles.)

➤ What does theatre communicate about these roles in contemporary, past, and even future settings?

Gender issues affect both female and male students whether they are aware of it or not. Directors of school theatre programs, therefore, should be aware that the choices they make about dramatic material convey undeniable messages about gender issues. Various "classic" plays may have limiting portrayals of gender roles. The sad truth is that most plays from all periods of theatre history have more male roles than female roles while theatre programs often have more female students than male students. For instance, a number of classic comedies, including those of Shakespeare and Molière, conclude with female protagonists attaining marriage as their ultimate goal. Of course, you should not interpret this observation as discouraging you from producing historically significant works of dramatic literature with your students. Rather, consider how gender roles are presented in plays you explore with students and how your work with young people might encourage them to think critically.

Teachers can draw on school resources to build historical and cultural contexts for their students' experiences with dramatic material of any period. The study of social history becomes particularly vital when a play includes narrow treatment of diversity and gender issues. For example, when dealing with *As You Like It* (or any Shakespeare play), it is important for students to know something of the social and political world of Renaissance England, including the status of women and the fact that they were not allowed to act on public stages. The composition of Shakespeare's all-male acting company may have affected the preponderance of male roles in his plays. Resources you might consider to explore these issues include the school's media staff, judicious use of the Internet, print and film sources, and other faculty members, especially teachers in areas such as history, language arts, and visual and other performing arts.

Student Explorations   Perhaps the most potent source for considering gender issues relevant to adolescence may be the students themselves. Playwriting and devising experiences can yield meaningful opportunities for young people to explore gender issues through theatrical expression. One teacher invited students to write responses to various types of male and female roles encountered through improvisation and classroom study of plays. These students also completed various tasks that encouraged them to consider cultural expectations of gender roles, such as personal opinion surveys and analysis of media messages. During the same semester, these students also wrote their own plays, creating characters and plots driven by individual or group choices. After the original plays were created, the teacher asked students to write similar responses about gender roles, this time based on their own plays. When comparing the students' analysis of their original work with the earlier responses, the teacher saw numerous instances of young people creating original roles they perceived as more multidimensional than the male and female characters they previously encountered elsewhere.

Gender Balance   You may also consider what kinds of gender issues are explored when undertaking long-range planning. In making classroom curriculum choices as well as selecting extra- or cocurricular production material, cast a critical eye for balance and variety in playwrights, subject matter, roles, and historical periods. Are all of the plays to be explored in class and in productions written by playwrights of the same gender? Does every play end with a female character being rescued by a male character? The goal of this kind of questioning is not to suggest that there is anything wrong with a particular sort of play, playwright, or role. Instead, consider gender in a field of many critical issues surrounding diversity as you strive to provide balanced, quality learning opportunities for young people.

Consider, too, that issues of diversity and gender go beyond the theatre classroom; certainly they are broadcast in the choices made in the school production program. That is, the casting of plays as well as the selection of material to be presented are viewed by the school as a whole. The teacher's choices are manifest to the whole academic community, teachers and students alike. The potential exists for the thoughtful teacher to reflect the community in which she teaches and reinforce the value of diversity through the production program.

Your Way

The methods and learning activities that you employ as well as the procedures and expectations that you establish to explore the art and craft of theatre with your students are only as limited as your own imagination. Ultimately, the methods used will have varying degrees of success over time. Keep annotated records of what was used, the apparent success (or failure) in assisting students to achieve identified goals, and the timely ideas that occurred spontaneously as the lessons and activities progressed. Watching experienced teachers at work can prove to be very helpful to the beginning teacher. You may notice that the successful teacher typically commands attention through a serious and enthusiastic approach to her subject. She may also exhibit a confidence that allows her to admit what she does not know and the willingness to help the students find out. Regardless of the subject or the method used, little can replace the exuberance of a teacher who takes joy in her task and has a strong affection for theatre in the classroom.

EXTENSION ACTIVITIES

1. You will most likely have encountered information about student learning styles in your education courses and readings. Review your understanding of learning styles, and brainstorm a list of responses to the following questions: Which teaching methods might work well for any learning style? Which methods would not work effectively for certain learning styles? What particular tools does the theatre teacher have for maximizing student success with all learning styles? If you are not familiar with learning styles, conduct an Internet search for current material on this important topic.

2. Identify a particular lesson plan that you might teach in a theatre course for high school students. Based on the topic you have selected, try the following tasks:

   ➤ Identify one or two essential questions.

➤ Describe how you would employ one or more teacher-centered methods to develop this lesson plan.

➤ Explain how two or more student-centered methods would work well for this lesson plan.

3. With a partner, plan a thematically organized unit for a middle school theatre class. The unit may follow a pattern of reverse chronology or it may be cross-cultural. The finished document should be in the form of a lesson plan. It should include a list of support materials, student activities, resources, and a culminating activity and/or assessment. Present and discuss your thematic plan with the class on the assigned day.

4. Download a couple of lesson plans from ArtsEdge (see below). Study them to discover the instructional methods employed. Are they teacher-centered or student-centered?

STAY CONNECTED

Examine the lesson plans found on the Kennedy Center site, artsedge .kennedy-center.org/teach/les.cfm, then use the dialogue box to locate theatre as the subject and the particular grade level you are interested in. This site has many strong and innovative lesson plans. Keep going back to it to discover new postings.

Browse through the following site (maintained by a professor at James Madison University): www.artslynx.org/theatre. You'll find lots of topics including those on diversity.

HELPFUL HINTS

➤ **Explore Resources**   Plan and arrange to have your classes visit the school media center early in the term. Develop a scavenger hunt that allows the students to explore the facility and locate resources that pertain to the theatre topics that will be covered during the term.

➤ **Find Guidance**   Spend some time getting to know your guidance personnel and their procedure for identifying students' interests. They can become a valuable resource for helping you locate students who might have potential for your program.

➤ **Make Choices**   When using a movie as support material, consider showing only the pertinent or significant scenes (for example, the ballet sequence from *Oklahoma!*), rather than the whole film. Often, students will benefit more from a taste rather than the whole film, which in many cases may not be an effective use of class time.

➤ **Explore Diversity Issues**   Beginning teachers will benefit from connecting with current discussions in professional circles to learn about diversity issues, such as through subscribing to journals that explore theatre and education. You might also consider applying for professional development funding available in your area with the goal of attending national or international conferences. Many workshop sessions, speakers, and theatrical presentations at such events will broaden your perspective on the relationship between diversity and theatre education. Teachers can reap profound benefits from continually looking into new vistas to consider connections between arts education and diversity.

4

Assessment
Finding Out What They Know

Assessment is a label used by many education professionals, including those in colleges of education, state departments of education, and secondary school administration. However, everyone may not mean precisely the same thing when they use the term *assessment*. For the purposes of this discussion, assessment embraces two quite distinct components: *measurement* and *evaluation*.

Measurement Measurement tries to determine the extent of the student's growth or behavior over time in one or more of three areas: intellectual, emotional, and motor. Intellectual growth is the student's ability to think and know, to retain and integrate facts and concepts. Emotional growth is the student's affect in dealing with the world, sometimes called maturity. Motor growth is the student's ability to perform certain motor tasks. Like all teachers, the theatre teacher must become proficient in measuring each of these behaviors. When trying to gauge intellectual growth, for example, the teacher will determine the extent to which the student can compare and contrast basic actor-audience relationships. Or, when attempting to calculate emotional growth, for instance, the teacher will discover the extent to which the student can work in groups or accept direction and criticism on a class project. When endeavoring to measure motor growth, for example, the teacher will register the student's ability to learn choreography or blocking.

For some, measurement means only testing. Surely, tests can be immensely valuable measurement instruments. There are, however, other ways to appraise a student's intellectual, emotional, and motor growth. In fact, the current climate in arts education recognizes that formal tests—objective and essay tests—may not be the best way to measure "make" and "do" projects, that is, individual and group performances, improvisational

66

exercises, design projects, creative portfolios, journals, and the like. Instruments such as checklists and rubrics are much more appropriate to these activities.

Evaluation *Evaluation* is a term almost synonymous with alphabetic grades. It is the value judgment, or interpretation, a teacher gives to the measurement scores. A letter grade may look simple on a report card, but the astute teacher knows how difficult it is to assign that grade as the alphabetic evaluation distills a lot of information into a potent symbol, especially at the end of a formal grading period.

Suppose a student is awarded 36 out of 50 points on the performance of a monologue. What does the number 36 mean in this instance? How does the teacher interpret that number? If it was the highest number in a class of twenty-five, it may indicate superior work (an A). If it was the lowest number awarded, the judgment is bound to be quite different. And what about the *student* who was awarded the score of 36? If this is the best work the student has done to date (a subjective evaluation), to what extent will the alphabetic grade be influenced by this information? The answer will depend on the teacher's philosophy, the school's policies, and the district's mandates.

Perhaps the example will be clearer if we say that the same student has earned 80 points out of a possible 100 points on an objective test. Is the score of 80 more valid or reliable because the test is thought to be more "objective"? This issue, along with others, will be encountered later in this section.

What to Assess?

Assessment is linked to objectives. Superior teachers relate assessment to desired student outcomes. These teachers decide beforehand what students should know or be able to do at the end of a unit and course. Then, they choose instruments to assess these outcomes. It might be helpful at this point to review Chapter 2, especially the sections on student outcomes.

Why Assess?

Assessment, accumulating information about a student's progress and then appraising that information, is a tool of immense value to a number of constituencies. The teacher's assessment of a specific student, or a group of students, is carefully noted by students themselves, their parents, teachers, administrators, and the school district. In short, assessment serves many masters.

Students   It is a fact of life that grades, a translation of assessment into a numerical or alphabetic certainty, are vitally important to students. Students use the teacher's assessment of their work on a daily, weekly, unit, and term basis to check their mastery of the subject matter. They want to know how well they did on their design project for *The Crucible*, or how well they performed in a scene. In addition they want to know if they are progressing at a satisfactory level, if they will make the honor roll, pass the course, advance to the next grade level, or if they will earn some sort of scholarship when they enter college. Most students are also motivated by earning a good grade. It gives them a sense of accomplishment if the teacher judges their work to be excellent.

Parents   Parents are sometimes more concerned with the periodic assessment of their children found on a report card than they are with their child's daily work. Report card assessment tells them, in a time-honored shorthand, how their children are doing over a long time span. Like some students, some parents are obsessed with whether their child made an A or B. If the grade is lower, the teacher may hear from these parents.

Teachers   Teachers use assessment in a variety of ways. On a daily or weekly basis, it lets them know if the material they are presenting is getting through to the class. Whether the class has been studying play structure or elements of theatrical design, for example, the assessment process will let the teacher know if the class as a group has assimilated basic concepts. If they haven't grasped the material, then the teacher must consider whether reteaching or a formal review is in order. If students have mastered the current material, then the teacher can be confident to move to the next unit of work.

Assessment also helps teachers discover the needs and abilities of their students. The truism is that every student is different. Teachers must determine how alike and how divergent their students' levels of achievement are. Teachers also use assessment to signal to the administration, parents, and student the degree to which the student has mastered the content of the course.

The theatre teacher needs to be especially vigilant and clear about assessment. Some parents and students believe assessment in the theatre classroom is a nebulous concept since the assessment of so much of the work will seem subjective. How, many may wonder, can a teacher differentiate between a superior design project and one that is average, or unacceptable? When studying performance, what does an A mean? How can a student make a D or an F in an acting class, a parent might ask? Some administrators have been known to ask the same questions. The discussion that follows may help you answer satisfactorily such questions.

Supervisors   Supervisors of fine arts programs may use the teacher's periodic assessments to discover whether the students are mastering the curriculum adopted by the school district or the state. Because assessments are widely disseminated, the beginning theatre teacher must appreciate and act on the demands that each constituency places on evaluation and grades.

The new theatre teacher must understand that assessment is making a judgment about a student's accomplishments (or lack of them). The more information the teacher has upon which to make that judgment, the more valid the assessment will be. The important precept is to assess regularly and often, using a variety of instruments. A good teacher will not base a student's unit grade, for example, on only a few assessments.

Assessing Performances, Design Projects, Playwriting, Improvisations, and Similar Activities

Projects such as the performance of scenes or monologues, design assignments, portfolios, and journals are "make" projects; they are creations that result in a product. Thus, the students *perform, exhibit, build, collaborate, write, invent.* Performances, design projects, scripts, portfolios, journals, and improvisations are best assessed by using checklists and rubrics rather than objective or essay questions.

When thoughtfully prepared, checklists and rubrics provide for a more standardized, less subjective evaluation. Both instruments allow the teacher to score the product according to a specified set of criteria, *and only those criteria.* Evaluation is thus more transparent to students and their families. These instruments can also help the teacher design the content and activities that culminate in the use of checklist or rubric, if they are devised and distributed as unit instruction begins.

Checklists and rubrics serve another important instructional purpose. They guide student learning. If the checklist or rubric is distributed to students as the instruction begins, they can serve as a study guide that answers the oft-asked question What are we supposed to do? or, How are we going to be graded? Checklists and rubrics, in short, are related measurement tools that will help students answer these and similar questions.

Checklists A checklist is a series of questions that reinforce what is required of the student. These questions should convey the criteria that the teacher will use to assess a product, be it the set design for a play, a performance project, or the direction of a scene or a short play. Study the ground plan assignment and checklist (Figure 4–1). Is the assignment clear? Does the checklist flow from the assignment? Are the questions reasonable? How would you adapt this document for use in the school and grade level to which you are assigned?

Ground Plan Assignment

Directions: Devise a ground plan for the play you have selected for an imaginary production in our Little Theatre. Be sure to review your class notes and the textbook before you begin. Use the ground plan checklist to help remind you of the important elements inherent in a sound ground plan.

Ground Plan Checklist

➤ Will the ground plan fit the stage of our Little Theatre?

➤ Is the ground plan, including all set pieces, in the appropriate scale?

➤ Is the stage arrangement balanced and focused?

➤ Are the entrances and exits placed in such a way that they support the script?

➤ Can the audience easily see all of the stage areas?

➤ Is the drawing neat and readable?

➤ Is the drawing clearly labeled?

Figure 4–1 By devising this checklist, the teacher has communicated to students the assessment criteria and outlined much of the content of the unit. To teach the concept of *scale* the teacher might first have the class measure the Little Theatre and then make a master ground plan for the space in an appropriate scale—usually $\frac{1}{2}'' = 1'$ or $\frac{1}{4}'' = 1'$.

The ground plan checklist is a clear statement of what the teacher should have taught prior to asking students to complete the ground plan assignment. It is, in short, an outline for the ground plan unit. For that reason, the efficient teacher will formulate learner outcomes for "make" or "do" standards (National Content Standards 1 through 4, for example), devise the assessment vehicles, and then construct an appropriate checklist (or rubric) for each of the unit's undertakings. When this planning is completed, the teacher has dictated in the checklist(s) and rubric(s) the kinds of learning activities that will be needed for that unit.

The very questions that make up the ground plan checklist can be turned into a measurement instrument by adding a simple *yes* or *no* after each question (Figure 4–2).

Ground Plan Assessment Checklist		
Criteria	Yes	No
Will the ground plan fit the stage of our Little Theatre?		
Is the ground plan, including all set pieces, in the appropriate scale?		
Is the stage arrangement balanced and focused?		
Are the entrances and exits placed in such a way that they support the script?		
Can the audience easily see all of the stage areas?		
Is the drawing neat and readable?		
Is the drawing clearly labeled?		

Score: Each Yes earns one point for a total of 7 points.
Figure your score by dividing 7 into the points you earned.

Figure 4–2 Note that either the criterion was met or it was not met. This yes/no checklist does not recognize degrees of accomplishment.

This preceding checklist does not allow the teacher to award partial credit for any of the seven criteria; it's all or nothing. Perhaps the student "almost always" labeled elements of the ground correctly. A way to recognize partial credit for a less than perfect performance is to weight the checklist.

Weighted Checklists A *weighted checklist* is a scoring tool that incorporates the evaluative criteria of a checklist with a scoring component that will allow the teacher to differentiate levels of performance. Because of its flexibility, a weighted checklist can be a very potent measurement tool. For example, if the teacher believes that some criteria are more central than others, then those criteria can be weighted more heavily than others. It also allows the teacher to award "partial credit." Note the changes made in transforming a standard checklist into a weighted checklist (Figure 4–3).

Ground Plan Assessment			
Criteria	**Possible Score**	**Score**	**Comments**
The ground plan is designed for use in our theatre.	20 points		
The drawing, including all set pieces, is in the same scale, including the furniture.	15 points		
The stage arrangement is balanced and focused.	15 points		
The entrances and exits are effectively placed to support the script.	10 points		
The audience can see all of the stage areas easily.	10 points		
The drawing is neat and easily readable.	10 points		
The drawing is correctly labeled.	10 points		
Total points			

A total of 90 points can be earned.
Figure your score by dividing 90 into the points you earned.

Figure 4–3 The weighted checklist can be a valuable teaching tool by pointing out to students that some criteria are more significant than others.

Here's another example. The following weighted checklist might be used in a directing unit.

Directing Scene Assessment			
Criteria	**Possible Score**	**Score**	**Comments**
The ground plan for the scene is helpful to the staging.	15 points		

The actors are secure in their lines, blocking, and business.	25 points		
The scene seems to gain momentum as it progresses.	25 points		
The blocking helps convey the dramatic action.	15 points		
The given circumstances are acted upon.	15 points		
The actors are compelling in telling the playwright's story.	25 points		
Total points	120 points		

A total of 120 points can be earned.
Figure your score by dividing 120 into the points you earned.

Figure 4–4 Note in the preceding checklists and in the rubrics that follow, students are required to figure their own scores as a percentage of a perfect score. This technique helps to incorporate another discipline into the theatre classroom. Realize, too, all effective checklists and rubrics depend on the teacher developing sound criteria.

Rubrics The term *rubric* is a measurement tool used to determine a student's progress in accomplishing a given task. Usually in the form of a chart, a rubric reflects the objectives and learning outcomes of a lesson or unit, especially of made products like performances and projects. In essence, the rubric transforms the checklist into a measurement instrument by using the checklist criteria and then creating levels of student mastery. These levels, when clearly and succinctly stated, provide students with information about the degree of their success. For example, using the first criterion found in the ground plan checklist (Figure 4–1), four levels of mastery are created as described below.

Criteria	Level 1	Level 2	Level 3	Level 4
The ground plan fits on our stage.	More than one part of the set is well offstage.	At least one part of the set is offstage.	Everything fits but it's a tight, crowded fit.	The entire set fits easily on our stage.

Figure 4–5 In all well-constructed rubrics each level of accomplishment is specifically described in relationship to the listed criteria. If the teacher wishes, there could be five or six levels of mastery, depending on the needs of the assignment.

Clearly, one significant difference between the weighted checklist (Figures 4–3 and 4–4) and the rubric is that the rubric includes the comment that the teacher must provide in the weighted checklist. Rubrics, like weighted checklists, provide a score. The second line of the rubric begun in Figure 4–5 might include the following descriptors of student work.

Criteria	Level 1	Level 2	Level 3	Level 4
Everything on stage is drawn to the same scale.	The use of scale is inconsistent.	Several set pieces are in a different scale.	One or two set pieces are in a different scale.	The entire set and all set pieces are in a consistent scale.

Figure 4–6 Note that the levels of achievement are described in language that avoids such overworked subjective and adjectives as *good, bad, poor, excellent.*

This ground plan rubric, as you have noted, is constructed with four levels of discrimination, suggesting that 4 is the highest score for each of the ground plan criteria. But if one or more of the criteria is deemed less significant than others, then only two or three levels of performance could be used.

Criteria	Level 1	Level 2	Level 3	Level 4
The drawing is neat and readable.	The drawing is difficult to read.	While easily readable, the drawing is somewhat messy.	The entire drawing is neat and readable.	
The drawing is clearly labeled.	Many elements of the drawing are not labeled.	Most elements of the drawing are clearly labeled.	All elements of the drawing are clearly labeled.	

Figure 4–7 **Using the ground plan criteria found in the checklist, write the levels of achievement for the remaining four criteria. In this example, the highest number of points a student could earn would be 3. In the two previous examples, 4 points could be earned.**

Some tips in constructing checklists and rubrics include the following.

➤ Align the criteria with content standards.

➤ Confine the criteria to the essentials that match the unit or lesson's learner objectives.

➤ Make sure that the directions for the project match the listed criteria.

➤ Limit the levels of proficiency for each criterion to no more than six. Four or five levels are more manageable.

➤ The levels of proficiency should center on descriptions of achievement rather than focus on the limitations of the student's work.

➤ Descriptors within a criterion should be parallel in each level.

Rubric For a Duet Acting Scene					
Student's Name					
Criteria	**Mastery Level 5**	**Mastery Level 4**	**Mastery Level 3**	**Mastery Level 2**	**Mastery Level 1**
Memorization	All of the lines were memorized.	Almost all (or most) of the lines were memorized.	There was some stumbling for lines.	Fewer than half the lines were memorized.	The actor carried the script and read the lines.
Volume	Could be heard for the entire scene.	Could be heard for almost all of the scene but some lines were mumbled.	Volume was a problem much of the time.	Could be heard rarely but overall the presentation was inaudible.	Could not be heard.
Articulation	All words clearly articulated and thus clearly understood.	Most words clearly articulated but there were a few moments that were unclear.	Some of the words were clearly articulated and clearly understood.	The articulation was unclear for most of the scene.	Not understandable because of articulation.

Criteria	Mastery Level 5	Mastery Level 4	Mastery Level 3	Mastery Level 2	Mastery Level 1
Clarity of dramatic intention	The character's wants and needs were clear.	Most of the character's wants and needs were clear.	Some of the character's wants and needs were evident.	Hardly any of the character's wants and needs were clear.	The character seemed to be without wants and needs.
Movement	Used appropriate movement(s) and gestures.	Used mostly appropriate movements and gestures.	Used some appropriate movements and gestures.	Used inappropriate movements and gestures.	Used no or minimal movement.
Character development	Created a fully developed character and remained within that character for the full scene.	Created a developed character. Acted within that character for the full scene.	Developed a character but did not stay within its confines for the full scene.	There was little character development.	There was little or no evidence of creating a character.

Figure 4–8 This rubric for a duet scene has five levels of mastery with the levels in the reverse order; that is, the highest level is at the left and the lowest mastery level is at the right. In what ways does this rubric meet the tips for rubrics and checklist that were previously listed?

Portfolios and Journals Portfolios and journals are long-term assignments, probably the longest term assignments given to individual students to complete. The advantages of portfolios and journals include providing students with an opportunity to integrate their theatre knowledge, demonstrating creativity and writing ability, developing skills in organizing diverse materials in logical order, and learning to plan and complete a major long-term product. The assessment instruments for portfolios and journals must take into account the relative free-form nature of these types of assignments.

Portfolios have been used by professional theatre and visual artists for hundreds of years. Theatre designers, actors, and directors have collected samples of their best work, arranged them in a meaningful way, and placed them in some kind of carrying case—the portfolio—in order to transport them from job interview to job interview. Portfolio literally means "portable carrying case."

A portfolio need not be delivered in a carrying case in this technology-inspired age. The delivery vehicle can be via website or DVD. An excellent example of a Web-delivered design portfolio is one by the professional stage designer Jim Hunter (www.jimhunterdesigns.com).

The financial industry has used the term to mean a collection of an individual's investment instruments—stocks, bonds, mutual funds, and the like. Higher education uses the portfolio as a physical demonstration of learning in a particular field. For example, Olivet College began a portfolio program in 1995 to orient the college away from *what they teach* to *what students learn*. Olivet students are now required to present a portfolio to demonstrate higher-order learning and noncognitive learning. Many colleges and schools of education are now requiring portfolio demonstration of learning in their graduate programs.

It is clear that educators see the portfolio as a valuable type of assignment. They use the term to include at least the following qualities:

> ➤ A systematic collection of "things" or "items." Some educators refer to the collection as "artifacts." The artifacts may be videotapes, CDs, DVDs, drawings, photographs, audiotapes, writing samples, or any combination thereof.

> ➤ The items are carefully edited. That is, only the best representations of the student's work are included in the collection.

> ➤ The items are arranged in such as way as to tell a specific story, be it a process of learning, a collection of short plays by genre, or an exhibition of designs.

> ➤ The purpose of the collection is to demonstrate ability or accomplishment.

A portfolio assignment can be designed to serve many goals. A team might research a particular topic and present the results of the investigation in a portfolio. Or, a student may "direct a play on paper" by presenting documents that demonstrate play analysis and interpretation, directing strategies, notes for the actors and designers, or even a full set of costume plates and set and lighting renderings.

Journals can describe a number of things. They can refer to a bookkeeping ledger, a daily newspaper, or a kind of diary, for example. Educators use the term to describe a teaching method to foster written expression that also serves as an assignment to document and demonstrate higher-order learning. The journal—in the sense of diary—can take many forms. It may ask students to

> ➤ react to events, such as student or professional performances
> ➤ list critical terms and their meaningful definitions
> ➤ explore concepts or essential questions that the teacher posts through the semester

Journals are usually unedited documents. That is, entries are not finished essays. Depending on the teacher's preference, the writing may be informal (sentence fragments are acceptable) or formal (complete sentences). After a specific journal assignment, usually to continue throughout the semester, the teacher collects the journals periodically to assess the student's progress.

Assessing Journals and Portfolios   The portfolio and journal are assessed by a using a rubric or checklist that is directly related to the assignment. The assessment instrument and the assignment should be distributed to students in writing at the same time.

Acting Journal Assignment

Directions: All of the following three entries are to be completed in your journal by the end of each week.

Response entry: Analyze a theatrical performance you experience in class, either live (that is, the work of other students) or on film.

Process entry: Describe the steps you take to prepare your individual presentation of various roles for class. Evaluate the usefulness of at least one of the steps as part of this description.

Prompt entry: Respond to teacher questions as posted each week on the journal section of the bulletin board.

Assessment checklist:

75% = Content

Are the ideas fully developed? Could the ideas be understood by someone who is not taking this class?

Are points supported with specific examples? Are the examples adequately described?

Is each entry concise? That is, does each entry explore the topic effectively without unrelated material or undue repetition?

Does the analysis demonstrate depth of thought? Over the course of the semester, does the analysis become more acute as the student gains in experience and theatre knowledge?

25% = Form

Do the mechanical errors distract from the meaning of the entry?

Is each entry three quarters of a page in length (typed, 12 point font, double spaced)?

Are there headings that give the student's name, date, type, and title of entry?

Are the entries completed on schedule?

Figure 4–9 If you were a student reading this assignment and its accompanying checklist, would you know what was expected of you?

The following portfolio assignment and checklist may serve as a model for a other portfolio assignments.

Portfolio Assignment: Playwriting	
Directions: At the end of this unit, you will have completed the following items to include in your playwriting portfolio.	
Portfolio Items	**Date Completed and Included in Portfolio**
Worksheet on playwriting format (to include at least three examples of stage directions and of dialogue).	
Brainstorming documents (based on brainstorming activities experienced in class).	
Character analysis: Brief description of all of the characters in your play. Detailed analysis of two or more characters based on the handout distributed in class.	
Description of Setting: One or more paragraphs describing the setting for your play in detail. Five or more visual images that represent your play's setting, including both original sketches and photos or drawings from magazine or other sources.	

Portfolio Items	Date Completed and Included in Portfolio
Early draft of your original one-act play (with revision marks from your teacher as well as at least one peer editor).	
Final draft of your original one-act play (typed in playwriting format to be practiced in class).	
Playwright's reflection: Write a letter to future playwrights in this class. What did you find rewarding about the experience of playwriting? What would you do differently if you were to write a play again?	
Extra credit: Create a program and a poster for your play. If your play were produced, who would act the roles? Where and when would it take place? What advertising logo and graphics would best describe your play?	

The following checklist will be used to assess the playwriting portfolio.

Weighted Checklist for Playwriting Portfolio		
Portfolio Item	Points Awarded	Possible Points
Worksheet on playwriting format		12
Brainstorming documents		15
Character analysis		25
Description of setting		25
Early draft		40
Final draft		60
Playwright's reflection		20
Extra credit: poster and program		10
Evaluation of process: Are the parts of the portfolio related to each other, leading to the final draft and reflection?		25

Total points possible: 225 (235 points with extra credit option)

Figure 4–10 Can you construct a portfolio rubric based on this checklist?

Assessing Intellectual Progress: Objective and Essay Tests

Objective and essay tests are ideal instruments to measure students' cognitive behavior. In short, they measure knowledge as well as comprehension, analysis, and the ability to synthesize.

Objective Tests Every college student has experienced the four most popular types of objective questions: multiple-choice, true-false, completion, and matching. Objective items, with the exception of completion items, measure the student's ability to *recognize* the best answer; students are not required to remember information. That is, multiple-choice, true-false, and matching items seldom measure recall, the student's ability to *recollect* information or concepts, as these selected-response items have the answer incorporated in the item.

Objective tests are like a shotgun blast. Each question is a single pellet. The more pellets in the shotgun shell, the better the target area is covered. The same is true of an objective test—the more items, the better the student's mastery of the subject matter can be measured. Only a teacher in a specific situation can determine if there are enough items in the test to cover the material, but clearly a ten-item multiple-choice test can't possibly cover much material. That's why national objective tests, like the SAT, include so many questions.

The most powerful advantage of objective test formats is that the questions can measure a wide range of material in a very short time because the student's answer is preselected by the response options included in the question. Because of these factors, objective tests can be quickly administered and speedily scored.

Some general tips for making good objective tests, no matter the question format, include the following:

➤ Each test item should be clear and unambiguous.

➤ The language level should be simple and clear enough for all students to understand.

➤ Use a variety of test formats but group like formats together. For example, all true-false questions should follow one another.

➤ Make sure all of the content taught is covered by the test. If one tenth of available class time was devoted to a particular topic, the teacher must try to ensure that about one tenth of the questions are devoted to that same topic.

➤ The entire test should be easy for the most prepared and difficult for a student who is poorly prepared.

> ➤ Construct the complete objective test well in advance so that it can be set aside and read later for grammar, syntax, clarity, and ambiguity.

There are no nationally endorsed objective theatre arts tests available. However, many secondary school textbooks have test banks available in the supplementary materials that the publisher provides the teacher. The beginning teacher may want to take advantage of this timesaving source of test questions. As the years go by, teachers can develop their own bank of questions specifically geared to the material they are teaching, the individual's teaching style, and the emphasis they are placing on certain topics.

The examples of objective question formats that follow will model the preferred form of the questions, provide clear directions to the student for answering each question format, and offer some practical tips on constructing valid questions.

Matching Test Items   Matching questions are perhaps the most interesting of all objective items for both teachers and students. For the instructor, matching items can be stimulating to write, almost like constructing a puzzle. Students seem to find them more challenging than other types of objective items.

There are three parts to matching items, the directions and two columns of items to be matched. (See Figure 4–11) The student is required to connect relationships. One significant advantage of matching questions is that wild guessing is reduced if there are more items in column B than in column A. If choices are intended to be used more than once, the directions should so indicate.

Directions: Match the playwrights or actors in column B with the dates of their life found in column A. Note: Three of the entries in column B will not have matching dates.

Column A	Column B
*1897–1975	1. Shakespeare
*1564–1616	2. Sophocles
*1622–1673	3. Molière
* 525–456 B.C.	4. Aeschylus
	5. Thomas Betterton
	6. Thornton Wilder
	7. David Garrick

Figure 4–11 The basic form of this question might be used for a final exam on theatre history. The asterisk represents the question number that would correspond to the same number on an answer sheet.

Tips for writing matching test items include the following.

> ➤ To help avoid confusion, all of the material in columns A and B should be on the same page of the test.
> ➤ Limit column B to ten or fewer entries.
> ➤ The material in both columns should be clearly related. Note that in the previous example, all entries in column A are dates and entries in column B are important playwrights or actors.
> ➤ The directions should identify the relationship between the columns. Study the directions listed in the previous example.

Multiple-Choice Items   These test items are the most prevalent format in standardized tests, even though they are the most difficult to write. A multiple-choice item is made up of two parts, a *stem* (the first part of the item) and the *response options* that will complete a statement or answer the question posed in the stem. See the sample question in the box below. Most often the item takes the form of completion where the stem presents an incomplete statement that the response options will complete.

Multiple-choice items mitigate against the student wildly guessing the correct answer, especially for those questions that provide five response options.

Directions: Select the choice that best completes the thought or statement.

* A lighting designer wanting to color light would probably use a
  1. pattern
  2. silhouette
  3. section
  4. plot
  5. gel

Figure 4–12 This completion multiple-choice question might be used for a unit exam on lighting. The asterisk represents the question number that would correspond to the same number on an answer sheet.

The stem of a multiple-choice item can also pose a question while the response options provide the correct answer. The question in Figure 4–13, perhaps suitable for a test on acting or directing, illustrates this form of the question.

Directions: Select the choice that best answers the question.

*If you are in the audience, what is the area of the stage called that is closest to you and on your left?

1. upstage right
2. upstage left
3. downstage right
4. downstage left

Figure 4–13 A series of multiple-choice questions like this one or the one in Figure 4–12 may appear easy to construct. In reality, these items are time-consuming to write.

Tips for constructing multiple-choice items include the following:

➤ Have at least four response options. Avoid using fewer than three response options. Five choices are better than four.

➤ Avoid "all of the above" or "none of the above" as response options. If students can identify one response option that is clearly false, then they will know that the "all of the above" response is also incorrect. The reverse is true of the "none of the above" response option.

➤ The stem should be clear and complete.

➤ The response options should be parallel in construction, length, and content.

➤ The correct responses should be distributed so that they appear equally placed throughout the test in all positions—1 2 3 4 5.

➤ The incorrect response options, called *distractors*, should be plausible. Avoid using fanciful or obviously incorrect response options.

➤ The stem should be stated positively. Avoid negative statements as they can confuse even the better students.

➤ Response alternatives should be about the same length so as not to tip the right answer or lead the student to select the incorrect response options.

True-False Items This familiar objective format asks that the student judge a statement for accuracy, to decide whether it is either correct or incorrect. <u>The ideal true-false statement should identify a concept and an attribute associated with it.</u> The concept is truly phrased but the attribute may or may not be true. See the example that follows. The drawback to this format is that, statistically, students who guess should be able to get half of the questions correct. The following sample question might be used to measure learning in a unit on acting.

Directions: Read the following statement. If you believe it is true, write a *T* on the answer sheet; if you believe the statement is false, enter an *F*.

*The term *given circumstances* means the playwright must provide the actor with the major details of a play.

Figure 4–14 Study this question. Is it written in accordance with the following tips? What about the questions found in Figures 4–12 and 4–13?

Tips for writing true-false items include the following.

➤ Avoid negative statements. If you must use a negative be sure to call it to the student's attention by some typographical means—<u>underline</u>, **boldface**, *italics*, all CAPITAL LETTERS, or some combination of these examples.

➤ Use approximately the same number of true responses as false ones.

➤ Avoid incorporating the exact language of the text into the statement. Students think these text quotations are "picky." More importantly, however, such quotes tell students the teacher prefers rote learning rather than independent thinking.

➤ Don't use qualifiers like *all, none, always,* or *never.* These specific determiners suggest that the statement is likely to be false.

A variation of the true-false format asks the student to explain why a statement was judged false. This compelling modification of the familiar format is more time-consuming to score as the student's response is not limited to a true-false judgment. However, it will tell the teacher much more about the mastery of content. This spin on the format can also be used to provoke discussion after the quiz. This type of question, illustrated in Figure 4–15, is a stepping-stone to the essay test.

Directions: Read the following statement. If you believe it is true, write a *T* on the blank by the statement; if you believe the statement is false, enter an *F*. If you judge the statement to be false, briefly explain *why* the statement is false in the space provided after each statement.

_____ *The term *given circumstances* means the playwright must provide the actor with the major details of a play.

_____

_____

_____

_____

_____

Figure 4–15 This variation of the true-false format can let the teacher see the student's thinking process.

Completion Items These items call for the student to fill in the blank with a word or phrase that correctly completes the sentence. Thus, completion items require recall rather than recognition. Completion items cannot be mechanically scored because the answer provided by the student may take several forms. It is not, in short, a selected-response item. The following are examples of completion items.

Directions: Fill in the blanks with the word or phrase that best completes the sentence.

* The vertical support in a flat is called a _____.
* The piece that secures the toggle bar to the stile is called a

  _____.

* The two most important qualities of light are
  _____ and _____.

Figure 4–16 Note that the completion items are short and unambiguous.

Tips for writing completion items include the following.

> ➤ For clarity and to avoid student confusion, limit the blanks to no more than two per item.

> ➤ Word the item so that only one answer is correct.

> ➤ Construct the sentence so that the blank(s) come at the end, or very near the end, of the sentence. Never start a completion item with a blank.

> ➤ Again, avoid quoting directly from the textbook.

Essay Tests   Essay items more accurately measure higher-order intellectual processes than do objective items. Although objective items most often measure *recognition* almost exclusively, essay items require the student to *organize, integrate, consolidate,* and *synthesize*. Essay questions compel students to recall information as well as to arrange that information in some meaningful way within the boundaries set forth in the question. That is, students are asked to *compare, describe, evaluate, interpret, justify, list and explain, trace,* or *contrast* using their own wording.

Like all test items, essay questions have advantages and disadvantages. Essay items can be quickly written by the teacher but are time-consuming to grade. Although an objective item should have only one incontrovertible answer, an essay test should be capable of being answered in several ways. Hence the teacher must spend time discerning the student's train of thought, understanding the argument, and discovering if the student omitted critical areas of knowledge requested in the question. Some students, even the most prepared, will have difficulty with essay questions if they write methodically and slowly. Perhaps they can't organize material adroitly. Perhaps their motor skills are not fully developed, or maybe they are used to using a computer keyboard rather than composing a handwritten response.

Essay items can be brief, requiring only a short paragraph to answer, or they can necessitate a longer, more detailed response. Test theory suggests that a cluster of short essay questions are more likely to have *content validity* (defined on p. 91) as they cover the subject matter much like the shotgun blast described earlier. It is difficult to cover course or unit objectives with one essay question.

An Essay Question Requiring a Somewhat Detailed Answer   The essay question either presents an imperative statement (List and explain the components of "given circumstances") or a problem (How would you go about discovering the "given circumstances" in a play in which you are playing an important part?).

The essay item found in Figure 4–17 dictates that students limit the scope of their answers and suggests a time limit so they may astutely budget the time spent on the item. It also lets students know that the answer should be a full essay not just an outlined response. These directions are intended to focus students on what is central to the response.

Directions: Using complete, grammatically correct sentences, answer the following question. Allot no more than fifteen minutes to this question.

Compare and contrast the plays of Aeschylus with those of Molière by identifying and briefly discussing at least two significant ways in which the plays are alike and at least three ways in which they differ.

Figure 4–17 Directions are an important part of the question, as they guide the student's answer. Teachers should make sure the directions are clear, complete, and helpful to the student.

The teacher should not only write the question, but at the same time prepare an answer in outline form, called a *key*. The key found in Figure 4–18 is more complete than would be expected from any student in the class, especially in the time limit imposed. It does, however, summarize the material covered in the text, lectures, or discussions.

Key

Molière	Aeschylus
More characters	Limited number of characters
Generally light in tone	Quite serious in tone
Gender-specific casting	All male company
Middle-class characters	Royal characters
Specific setting	General setting
Many props	Few or no props

Both can have musical elements.
Both are males writing about females.
The plays of both writers are considered superior dramatic works.

Figure 4–18 A key, like the one above, can also provide the teacher with notes for a review session. Would you return this key with the essay you have scored? Why? Why not?

Short Answer Essay Questions. A series of essay items that require only short but precise answers can more fully reveal the extent to which the student has mastered the subject matter. The number of questions should, of course, correspond to the time available to take the test. If the test is to be administered during a forty-five-minute period, then obviously there should be fewer items than a ninety-minute class period would accommodate.

Directions: Answer the following five questions in complete sentences. Spend no more than five to eight minutes on each question.

* Name and describe two plays by Molière.
* Name and describe a play by Aeschylus.
* List and describe four sources that will reveal the given circumstances in a play.
* Diagram and briefly explain the basic areas of a proscenium stage.
* Explain briefly the theatrical highlights of David Garrick's career.

Figure 4–19 Several short answer essay questions, using this model, will reveal the student's breadth of knowledge. A single essay question will disclose the student's depth of understanding.

By comparing the examples found in Figure 4–19, based on questions already presented in this discussion, you can see that the same basic material can be measured by using various test formats.

The construction of the key for all essay questions will, of necessity, depend on the textbook used, the emphasis the teacher places on the material, whether or not the students have been assigned a play by each playwright, and other variables. But the teacher should construct a key by which each essay will be evaluated.

Tips for writing essay items include the following.

➤ Avoid writing open-ended questions such as "Discuss the plays of Aeschylus and Molière." This kind of a question invites scattershot, unthoughtful answers. It's akin to asking "Tell me everything you know about the plays of Aeschylus and Molière."

➤ Questions should limit the scope of the answer and direct the student's response.

➤ Students should be told how much time they should devote to each essay question. See the directions contained in Figure 4–19.

➤ Most measurement experts suggest that the student should not be offered choices of questions to be answered. That is, don't give the student the option of answering question A or question B. Experts remind that the goal is measurement. Thus all students' mastery should be measured by the same instrument.

Check and Double-Check

Tests can yield important information to all concerned with the student's progress. To make sure the information is valuable, teachers must make sure the measurement instruments are solidly constructed.

Reflect for a moment on this statement: "The questions used in this examination have been scrupulously researched by a team of subject matter experts. The answers have not. Poorly worded, ambiguous, misleading, and stupid questions are par for the course." This paraphrasing of a comic disclaimer on a popular radio quiz show, of course, should not apply to the questions any teacher writes for her unwitting students. It would be surprising, however, if even an experienced teacher had not devised a question or two that was poorly worded or ambiguous, nevermind misleading. A goal of this preceding section has been to lead the beginning theatre teacher to write clear, well-phrased, unambiguous questions that students will not consider misleading or ambiguous.

If, in the course of administering an exam, you discover (or students question) an objective item as inappropriate for whatever reason, you can agree to skip the scoring of that item. Or, if in the scoring of the objective items, you discover a question that is not adequately clear, it can be skipped in the scoring.

Content Validity and Test Reliability

All teachers want to write good tests, instruments that adequately cover the content of the material being examined and tests that reward students who have seriously studied the material. These two concepts are embodied in the terms *content validity* and *test reliability*. The discussion that follows is a significant reduction of the concepts embodied in these two terms as well as the broader field of testing and measurement. We hope beginning teachers, armed with this introductory discussion, will continue to learn more about this fascinating field.

Content Validity   No test can possibly ask all the questions identified with a particular subject, especially considering the time restraints of the exam period. So the test must be assembled from a sample of all those possible questions. The best practice is to write and select questions that reflect the material taught and the time devoted to that teaching. For example, if the teacher spent a week teaching five aspects of given circumstances and the test of that material examined only one of the givens, then students will complain, rightly so, that the exam didn't cover all the material they were taught.

Thus, the principle of content validity relates to a test's ability to include all of the important content, skills, and understanding inherent in a particular topic. In short, teachers must ask themselves, Did the test cover the basic material? no matter if the period of instruction was one week, an entire unit, a nine-week period, or a semester.

The best way to determine whether your test has content validity is to ask an expert or another teacher if the test adequately covers the subject matter. Another, more immediate, way to discover content validity is to listen to students' reaction immediately after the test. If you hear, "It didn't cover half the material I studied" then you know something may be amiss. But if you hear, "I studied all the right things," then you can tentatively assume that the content of the test was probably valid.

Test Reliability   If a test is not valid, then its reliability is immaterial. The principle of test reliability relates to how trustworthy and consistent a valid test is. The critical question asks: Is the test a reliable indicator of student achievement?

An analogy that highlights test reliability concerns a thermometer. If you take your temperature with a thermometer at nine in the morning and get one result, then take it again at eleven and get a result that is six degrees different, and then take it still again at two in the afternoon and get yet a third questionable result, you know your thermometer is not a reliable instrument to measure your temperature. The same is true of a particular test. It must be consistent and internally reliable through time.

Standardized selected-response tests (multiple choice, true-false, matching items), such as those constructed and administered by the Educational Testing Service, have had their reliability established over time. The questions on such standardized tests have been subjected to statistical analysis and that result is expressed statistically in the test manual. The label *standardized test* in fact implies that each item has been statistically analyzed for reliability.

Teacher-originated selected-response tests, especially those written by new teachers, will probably not have been statistically validated unless the teacher has had training in statistics. But there are other ways to analyze selected-response items, albeit less statistically valid ways. Yet the teacher can gain important information about whether students have comprehended essential information by analyzing the test questions. In true-false items, for example, the teacher should examine how many students answered true and how many answered false to each item. If the desired response to an item is true but two thirds or three quarters of the students answered false, then the teacher can conclude one of two possibilities: either the material needs to be revisited in a review session, or the item was poorly written.

In a multiple-choice item analysis, the teacher determines how many students selected each of the responses. Suppose there are five alternatives and six students selected the first four responses and only two students selected the fifth response, which the teacher keyed as the correct answer. As in the true-false example cited previously, the teacher is left with the same two possible conclusions. If she believes the material needs to be retaught, then a review is in order. If she decides that the multiple-choice item is poorly constructed, then the item must not be scored and should be recast before it is reused. The same analytical process applies to matching items.

Essay tests present another aspect of test reliability. The teacher's judgment must be consistent in scoring essay question(s). For example, the teacher may have essay questions from sixty students to score. Is the teacher's judgment of the first ten papers graded the same in the final ten papers? Or has the standard shifted due to fatigue or boredom? A good way for teachers to check their own judgment is to score a few papers at random and record the score on a separate sheet of paper. Then, after all tests are graded, compare the first scores with the second scores. If the scores are quite close, the teacher's judgment can be called reliable.

By attending to the reliability of her grading, the teacher is in step with the values and actions of the professionals in the field of testing. Take the example of the renowned Educational Testing Service (ETS), which recently discovered a problem with the scoring of an important teacher licensing exam. The test was given eight times in eight different locales to a total of about forty thousand people. The test was the same in each locale, only the graders of the essay questions differed. ETS noticed more low scores than usual in two administrations of the test. When they investigated, they found that the short essay questions in those particular two administrations were graded more stringently than they were in the other six administrations. When ETS rescored the essay question about 10 percent of the test takers had moved from failing to passing. This example is shared here to emphasize the importance of reliability of grading in any educational setting.

There can be many reasons for weak reliability in objective tests. Two of the most important are poorly written questions and tests that are too short. Research indicates that longer tests are a more reliable indicator of achievement than are shorter ones. Teachers should understand that a five-item true-false test is inherently unreliable as a measurement of a student's mastery of information.⏋

EXTENSION ACTIVITIES

1. Using a search engine, enter the phrase *Bloom's taxonomy* and revisit this important site. This time, download two or three short articles concerning his taxonomy. As a class define the classification of educational objectives. Then discuss ways in which Bloom's work can help you to better write tests and learner objectives for theatre students.

2. Divide the class into teams. Assign each team to read a different chapter in the theatre textbook you will likely use during your first year of teaching. Each team will then write ten objective questions and two short essay questions. Share the questions with the class and evaluate the questions for clarity and form.

3. Review this chapter to determine if you know the meaning of the following key terminology: *stem, response options, recall, recognition, content validity*, and *test reliability*.

4. Begin now to create rubrics and checklists. As the class continues, copy and share them with your classmates. By the end of the term you could have a valuable collection.

5. Divide the class into two teams. One team is charged with investigating test validity, the other is assigned reliability. Research these two terms and each team will teach the other team about their topic.

STAY CONNECTED

This site, www.stephenfoster.com/rubrics.pdf, sponsored by *Stephen Foster, The Musical*, contains an interesting array of rubrics. Although they're generally slanted toward music, many of them can be adapted to fit the theatre classroom. Browse around!

Explore go.hrw.com/resources/go_ss/teacher99/rubrics/RUBRIC33.pdf to discover what this site calls a "Skits and Reader's Theater" rubric. In reality what they call a rubric, this textbook calls a weighted checklist. The page is part of the quite respectable Holt, Rinehart, Winston publishing website. Herein lies an important lesson about using the Web: terminology is not precise. You may find that what one site calls a lesson plan is little more than a class activity, or that the lesson plan does not employ the format discussed in Chapter 2. Or that what is called a lesson plan is in reality a unit plan. Moral: Use your common sense and understand that the language of pedagogy is often imprecise.

The Chicago Public Schools has a wealth of fine arts rubrics that may be helpful. Search intranet.cps.k12.il.us/Assessments/Ideas_and_Rubrics/Rubric_Bank/rubric_bank.html and explore.

This is a rich site: www.emsc.nysed.gov/ciai/arts/pub/artsamptheater.pdf. Pages and pages of theatre assessment instruments, sample questions, and assignments sponsored by the New York State Education Department. Browse.

HELPFUL HINTS

➤ **Observe**   Request permission from your administration to sit in on other classes to watch experienced teachers. Ask to see their tests. Discuss with these teachers their philosophy of assessment.

➤ **Use the Internet**   Begin to explore useful Internet sites that pertain to the various aspects of theatre you expect your students to study. Keep a current list of the useful sites for student reference. Internet sites that can be accessed from school computers must be carefully selected because some sites are barred automatically by the system. Your media center colleagues can be of assistance identifying useful sites that are accessible.

5

Integrated Teaching Across the Curriculum
Assisting Discovery

There are many ways to teach and to learn. As you become more experienced—and more confident—in teaching young people, you will experiment with various learning strategies, embracing those that you feel comfortable with and those that help your students learn. This chapter contrasts a venerable teaching tradition with one of its many alternatives.

All of us are familiar with discipline-centered teaching and learning. After all, this model of instruction has been employed for centuries. You have surely experienced it in college. You had courses in a particular academic discipline, be it theatre, English, history, political science, or one or more of the sciences. The instructors in each of these courses were concerned almost exclusively with their own particular subject to the exclusion of others. For example, rarely does an undergraduate course in British history examine the music of the era being studied.

Discipline-centered instruction is best described as a vertical model of teaching. The goal is to learn about one particular subject in depth; the more courses you take in a field, the deeper is your command of the discipline. In college, when you have studied enough disciplines you are said to have met the particular graduation requirements of your institution. Your reward is an undergraduate degree with the study of a major content area. This same model is most often used in middle and high schools: a collection of specific courses equals a diploma.

Discipline-centered instruction is not necessarily an outmoded organizational model. It is particularly efficient and effective for professional graduate programs like law, business, architecture, engineering, and medicine, for example. On the undergraduate level, this vertical model has been practical and successful.

During the past few decades, however, many K–12 educators and administrators have been suggesting more curricular integration. They ask whether the vertical model of instructional organization should be the only approach used to educate students for the workplace and/or further schooling. These educators, endorsed by such organizations as the National Association of Secondary School Principals (NAASP), have been urging teachers to consider another model of instruction—a horizontal model of connectivity. In fact, the NAASP recommended that high schools integrate their curriculum to "emphasize breadth over depth of coverage."

This horizontal model of instruction may go by a variety of labels, including *integrated curriculum, interdisciplinary learning, inquiry, problem-based learning*, and *teaching across the curriculum*. There are probably other labels as well. No matter what the designation, this approach to learning is based on connecting disciplines through project- and problem-based assignments. *Teaching across the curriculum*, the term we use, means an instructional approach that transcends the boundaries imposed by traditional subject parameters. It is a holistic approach to learning that helps students understand the partnerships between disciplines. You more than likely experienced the horizontal approach to instruction in your K–12 schooling.

Perhaps the contrasting approaches to learning embraced by these models can be made clearer by studying Figure 5–1.

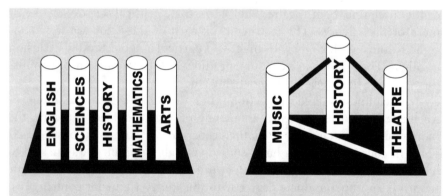

Figure 5–1 The model of instruction on the left illustrates discipline-centered instruction; the other drawing demonstrates the interdisciplinary instructional mode.

The terms *horizontal* and *vertical* learning were not intended to be used this way, but they can be seen as an architectural metaphor, as something approaching the post and lintel construction of a door. Vertical learning forms the posts and bridging those posts, creating a solid structure that will support weight, is horizontal learning. Together they make a doorway through which the student passes into mastery.

The strengths of vertical and horizontal teaching are many. This discussion is not meant to suggest the efficacy of one model over the other; they each have their place in the classroom. Indeed, students must first experience the discipline of theatre (vertical learning) before they can make connections with other disciplines (horizontal learning). That is, interdisciplinary instruction should never be viewed as a substitute for a strong grounding in the discipline itself. The Connecticut state education department expresses this dictum: "Interdisciplinary curriculum should be an expansion of, and not a substitute for, a sequential comprehensive curriculum in each subject discipline." In short, the most effective teachers make judicious use of both models, no matter what their discipline may be.

The chart in Figure 5–2 sets forth, in contrasting pairs, some of the most salient characteristics of the two models.

Vertical Model Traits		Horizontal Model Traits
Specialization	**vs**	Integration
Separation	**vs**	Synthesis
A silo of independence	**vs**	A beehive of connectivity
Distinct units of instruction abound	**vs**	Cross-curricular assignments are usual
Students work alone	**vs**	Students work with others
Facts reign	**vs**	Questioning of facts prevails
Answers govern	**vs**	Questions predominate
Names and dates dominate	**vs**	Ideas conquer

Figure 5–2 This chart summarizes the key descriptors associated with the vertical and horizontal models of instruction.

Five Horizontal Projects

To better understand how the features of horizontal model traits may be applied in the theatre classroom, study the five projects that follow. Set forth in differing detail, these problems are intended to illustrate central concepts of teaching across the curriculum.

Using Historical and Literary Explorations

This project can be assigned to the entire class. Ask each student to select and then research an important person studied in their history course. For example, Paul Robeson, Eleanor Roosevelt, Charles Lindbergh, Langston Hughes, Maya Angelou. or Jane Austen might be strong choices. Students are to document their research in a journal or portfolio.

When the research is completed, the students are then asked to develop a five-minute monologue using mostly the historical figure's own words. The student is encouraged to write transitional or introductory material in the voice of the particular person selected. Students may shape their monologues to answer a variety of questions. Some might include:

> ➤ Who am I?

> ➤ What did I do?

> ➤ Why did I think the way I did on a particular social/political issue?

> ➤ Why should you know my work?

The students are then to collect one or two costume and hand props that their research revealed were closely associated with the historical or literary celebrity. They are to memorize and present the monologue, with the theatrical accessories, as if that historical person were talking to the class. The teacher may wish to make the monologue performances available to other appropriate classrooms, particularly history and English classes.

As part of the introduction to this project, the teacher might show a section of a one-person play based on the life of a significant historical figure. One example might be the actor Hal Holbrooks' *Mark Twain Tonight* (available on DVD from Kultur). As an example of the research they might undertake, the teacher could also show a brief clip of Mark Twain himself as photographed by Thomas Edison; it is available on the web at www.hanni bal.net/twain. Similar material relating to other significant figures can be located on the Web. The class might practice brainstorming ideas for one sample person together, before beginning their individual projects.

For this project, particularly appropriate for grades eight to twelve, the teacher should allot a significant amount of class time to complete the investigations and fashion the scripts. (There can be no hard-and-fast rule as the length and frequency of class periods devoted to this project vary greatly from district to district. This caveat applies to the remaining sample projects.)

The teacher is not the source of information but a facilitator. She is a resource person, much as a librarian might be. In fact, library and computer research will be essential for successful completion of the project. In order for this literary or historical exploration to be effective, the teacher must develop student outcomes and a rubric spelling out how the student is to be assessed. A checklist would also be helpful to students to organize their assigned tasks.

What makes this project particularly effective is that it combines history, literature, social contexts, writing, technology, editing, scripting, organizing, and performing. The resulting performance will be a synthesis of a particular time and place in history or literature through one person's view. This project can cover content standards ❶ ❷ ❸ ❹ ❺ ❻ ❼.

Using Social Studies and Current Events

Divide the class into groups of four or five students. Each group is charged with writing one or two public service announcements (PSAs) that address a particular problem or issue facing their community. The project could begin with full-class discussions aimed at coming to grips with community problems: teenage smoking, recycling, preserving natural resources, or the large number of school dropouts. The more specific and local the problems are, the more motivated the students will be.

The public service announcement can be for radio, television, or newspaper. As part of the explanation of the project, the teacher may present models for each media. The final project for radio can be recorded and played to the class. The television PSA can be storyboarded with free-hand sketches or with digitally produced still pictures. Or if facilities are available, the PSA may be videotaped. The newspaper PSA might be computer-generated using clip art or actual photographs from archives or those taken by the group.

This project, too, will probably consume a significant amount of class time. Groups must have time to research the problem to be addressed, strategies for writing the PSA must be decided upon, and the actual product developed. The teacher may invite an advertising account executive to speak with the class and show products developed by the advertising agency.

Clearly this project will involve local current events, writing, organizing, working collaboratively, technology, scripting, media skills, as well as performing. If the teacher is thorough, the project could cover content standards ❶ ❷ ❸ ❹ ❺ ❻ ❼ ❽.

Using the Arts

This project is intended to demonstrate the interrelationship of the various art forms. The teacher presents the class with a portfolio of famous figurative paintings from the Renaissance on. There should be more pictures than students. If individual reproductions are not available, then the teacher should collect several art books, either devoted to a particular era or to a particular artist.

Students are to select a picture with figurative subjects that appeals to them. The students are then asked to select music contemporaneous with the painting that, in the students' opinion, expresses the mood or activity inherent in the picture. Then students are to explain in writing their choices along with a chronology that places in time the painting, the music, and other significant events that surround the era. They are then asked to write a five-minute play based on their selected painting, musical selection, and essay. Or, they may choose to choreograph a short dance, again using the painting, music, and essay. If a play is written, it should be cast and read to the class. If the student devises a dance, it should be performed.

In-class time must be set aside so that students can study the art books or individual reproductions, research the music of the period, make the musical selection, compose the scenario, and produce the play or dance. The teacher should require students to document their choices in their journals, including a chronology of the painting and the music. As in all project inquiries, the teacher must construct assessment rubrics, checklists, and related activities. With careful planning, this arts project could address content standards ❶ ❷ ❸ ❹ ❺ ❻ ❼ ❽.

Using Math

This problem may be particularly useful to the teacher as well as to the students. It involves devising a season of plays to be performed next year by students, including their plays' production budgets. Or, the problem could be more circumscribed by announcing a real or imagined season of plays and/or musicals at your school and asking the students to budget the productions. The teacher then would present the unorganized—but actual—raw expenses for a particular production or two that were staged at the school. The students would first be asked to organize those figures into appropriate categories: sets, costumes, lights, scripts, publicity, fees, and so on and present them as a cash flow statement. The resulting document would reveal the specific costs of such items as royalty and scripts, programs, advertising, and other costs that some students would not consider.

Using that statement as a model, the students then are to select one specific production and devise a realistic budget based on the program's past experience. The school bookkeeper might be a valuable resource person. He could demonstrate to the class what a cash flow statement might look like. Students would then present to the class their finding, describing the acting opportunities, including the number of roles for men and women as it relates to costuming, design needs, and estimated costs. Clearly, this project would reflect content standards ❸ and ❹ and could include ❺.

Using Physics and Math

Teams of students are formed to design on paper a section of a set for the balcony scene of *Romeo and Juliet*. The set piece could be original, designed by the students themselves, or one adapted from a photo of a famous production of Shakespeare's play provided by the teacher, or a combination of the two sources. Each of the teams would then devise plans to construct this particular set piece, first of metal and then of wood. Their plans should consider the load-bearing properties of the materials used and an estimate of the maximum load the balcony would be expected to hold. Each team would then present to the class the structural requirements of both media and the process that led them to their solutions. Clearly, this problem would require collaboration with a physics instructor or other structural expert. With some care this project could address content standards ❸ ❺ ❽.

Challenges Inherent in Project-Based Assignments

To prepare for these five endeavors, as well as all project- or problem-based learning, the teacher must clearly identify the theatre content standards that the assignment addresses. The teacher should also consider the content standards of the corollary discipline(s). Further, clear student outcomes must be identified as well as assessment instruments.

For the learning to be most effective and lasting, it is important that the completed assignment is presented to an audience that goes beyond the teacher. For example, the historical or literary project should ideally end in performance before other classes. The public service campaign assignment might be presented to the advertising executive who first introduced the project and agreed to return to the classroom for presentations.

The project that is undertaken must be genuine and not have a single predetermined solution. If the essential question is frivolous, then students will see work as frivolous. In short, the assignment must promote in-depth learning.

Teaching across the curriculum, as the five sample projects described previously illustrate, can be time-consuming. The teacher must set aside a sufficient block of time, using the school's scheduling system, to make sure students can comprehensively investigate the problem or project in some detail and depth. Moreover, the teacher must devote sufficient time to plan for the project or problem. For this reason, and others, it might be best if the beginning theatre teacher uses the interdisciplinary approach as a culmination to a yearlong course.

The Teacher and the School

Interdisciplinary curricula are devised and adopted by school administrators, either at the state, district, or school level. If your school district or individual school has developed interdisciplinary curriculum models, you should search out those documents and become familiar with their content. Such models will most likely set forth sample problems or projects, content standards, assessment rubrics, and perhaps sample lesson plans. But the beginning teacher should understand that although teaching across the curriculum has been endorsed by middle and secondary school educators and administrators, not all schools will have fully embraced this concept. If you find yourself in this situation, then you can demonstrate a willingness to work with teachers in other disciplines regardless of whether the district or the school has officially adopted an interdisciplinary approach to learning.

If your district does not have a developed interdisciplinary curriculum, then you can independently put this strategy into play in your own classroom. You can organize material and assignments in such a way that suggests to students that there is an interrelationship inherent in all disciplines. Or you might try implementing an interdisciplinary project with one other teacher, perhaps one in the fine arts area—dance, art, or music. In addition, you might identify some ways in which theatre arts might be incorporated into other disciplines.

EXTENSION ACTIVITIES

1. The Consortium of National Arts Education Associations has developed a pamphlet devoted to integrating arts education, "Authentic Connections: Interdisciplinary Work in the Arts." It can be found at www.naea-reston.org/pdf/INTERart.pdf. The URL is case sensitive. Download the publication and study it. Compare the approaches of the arts education consortium to teaching across the curriculum with the material presented in this chapter. Then, as a class, discuss the three models of interdisciplinary instruction: parallel instruction, cross-disciplinary instruction, and infusion.
2. The five examples of interdisciplinary projects found in this chapter could take up to several weeks of class time to complete. Working

with one other class member, invent an interdisciplinary assignment or two that would take only one or two class days to complete successfully. Each team should share their projects with the class.

STAY CONNECTED

Discover this site sponsored by Brigham Young University: www. byu.edu/ tma/arts-ed. You'll find a variety of topics, including unit plans and drama and theatre books. The section labeled "Improv Situations" is particularly useful.

HELPFUL HINTS

➤ **Join the Team**   Explore opportunities to work with members of other departments in order to create student experiences that support cooperative learning and cross-curricular activities.

➤ **Fine Arts**   If you are part of a fine arts department, find out what your colleagues are doing and what visions they might have for future projects that might include students from more than one art area, such as a schoolwide Fine Arts Festival.

➤ **Link to Other Disciplines**   Find out the format for writing formal essays, reports, and research papers from the English department. Include these requirements in your assessments of formal written assignments to help maintain consistency and high expectations across the curriculum.

➤ **Cooperate**   Find out what dramatic literature your students are studying in English class and what periods of history they will be covering in social studies. Your ability to introduce them to literature and information that support their studies in other classes can be very valuable to their learning experience.

➤ **Be Resilient**   Your personal goals for your students may involve project ideas that "haven't been tried before." Do not be discouraged. Often an idea is simply waiting for the right time.

6

The Teacher and School Productions—
Philosophical Considerations
Building Bridges

All theatre teachers eventually will be asked to provide performance opportunities for their students. Administrators, parents, and fellow teachers alike will expect the theatre teacher to devise ways for students to share their work meaningfully in public forums. These performances, of course, should unfold in ways that are connected to classroom learning and are appropriate for the students in a particular school. Such goals can be achieved through diverse routes, depending on the teacher, students, and the program.

New teachers, however, are best advised to set realistic and manageable goals for school productions, especially during the first year or so of teaching. There will be many responsibilities that require strong time management skills, such as classroom management, curriculum development, assessments, meetings, committee work, and professional development. There are also many things for a new teacher to learn about the school itself, the school district as an administrative unit, the school's administration, the faculty and staff, and, of course, the students themselves. Thus, beginning teachers are advised to think carefully and critically about what kind of production choices will support success in all areas of their new teaching position, not just the school production aspect of the job.

So, rather than dive headfirst into Mickey and Judy euphoria and shout to your students with enthusiasm, "Let's put on a show!" we urge you to first explore privately what kinds of production experiences you will endorse. Successful theatre programs can be built from many philosophical underpinnings. The teacher who reflects upon the nature of school productions that would be ideally suited to his students and environment can have a rich experience, if the particular school situation will allow a new teacher the luxury to act upon his theoretical musings. Before reaching a final conclusion, however, you should explore your new school's past.

Find Out What's Happened Before

Understanding and respecting the expectations that a certain community may have is critical. However, forming and articulating meaningful educational goals is also vital to a quality school production program. Whether your first teaching position is in a district with a long history of successful classroom and production programs or in a school where no theatre classes have previously existed, you will want to develop a clear philosophical approach to the issue of public performances and be able to support that position.

School production expectations may have been addressed during the interviews through which you were hired. There are often more subtle viewpoints that may arise later from the administration, the school community, the parents, and the students that will add to the challenges of developing a production philosophy that meets and extends the teaching standards and the public perceptions of all involved.

Discover those expectations early in your first year. Understand their implications. Of course, you are not usually bound to following such expectations; often, you can lead the school *eventually* in a new direction that will benefit the students and the program. Questions that the beginning teacher must ask herself (or others either directly or indirectly) to come to grips with the past that she inherits will include at least the following.

➤ What kinds of theatrical performances have been produced at the school in recent years, how frequently, for what audiences, and at what times during the academic calendar?

➤ Is the music department in charge of an annual musical? Is it the tradition for the theatre teacher to be involved? If so, in what capacity is she expected to serve? Is there a dance teacher on staff? Does she or one of her advanced students traditionally choreograph the musical? If the music department does not produce an annual musical, would they be willing to assist you in doing so in the coming years?

➤ Is there a tradition of student-directed and/or student-written productions?

➤ What roles and responsibilities have students taken in the preparations for productions during previous performance opportunities?

➤ Is the art department usually involved in creating the poster art or scenic elements for a production? If not, would this collaboration be a possibility?

➤ Does the school have an annual celebration of the arts? Does the school have a unit of history that is celebrated in a schoolwide festival, such as a Renaissance Fair, a Medieval Fair, Women's History Month, Black History Month, or a specific historical era such as the Roaring Twenties? How can you and your students become a part of these events in the coming years?

➤ Do the students, parents, and administrators expect the school to participate in statewide drama festivals? If so, what financial support is available?

Discovering the answers to these and similar questions will help direct your thinking about what kind of school production program you will be able to develop over the coming years. Having a clearly thought-out production philosophy will help you assimilate and process prior expectations, carefully steer the program in the direction you believe is best for the school and its students, and grow your program.

Your Production Philosophy

There are many valid philosophical approaches to developing school production programs. Possibilities include the following rather extensive listing:

➤ showcase of scenes and monologues for an invited audience featuring many students at different levels of experience with minimal technical support

➤ staged readings of original play(s) written by student(s) or the theatre teacher

➤ presentations by student improvisation group

➤ large cast performance of popular musicals like *Suessical*, *Annie*, or *The Music Man*

➤ full-length popular American plays like *Arsenic and Old Lace*, *Charlotte's Web*, or *Life with Father*

➤ an evening of one-act plays directed by students

➤ original performance created by an ensemble through group devising processes

➤ plays representative of a significant period in theatre history (for example, Greek tragedy, morality play, Shakespeare)

➤ productions of challenging material for a drama festival or competition with advanced students

> ➤ performance pieces with text, movement, and music inspired by oral histories and other primary sources on a significant aspect of a community's history
> ➤ plays for young audiences with performances for early childhood or elementary school audiences
> ➤ a mix of any of the approaches listed before

Many of the examples in the previous list vary greatly in technical requirements, the number of crew and actors required, expense, the specific requirements placed on the performance facility, and rehearsal time, among other factors. Arranging these productions in a continuum can reveal much about the philosophical underpinnings of each choice. Clearly some production choices are director-centered; they require that an experienced and well-trained director be at the helm. Others are student-centered. That is, the casts usually are small, the material is student written, and the technical requirements are minimal. Figure 6-1 represents such a continuum.

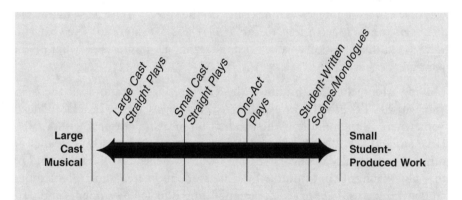

Figure 6–1 This continuum suggests several theoretical approaches. Consider the implications of this illustration. Director-centered productions are often the "supersized" musicals while student-centered productions tend to be smaller and less technically demanding.

At one end of the continuum is the large cast Broadway musical using sophisticated amplified sound, lighting, moving scenery, and lavish rented costumes performed in a large auditorium with a "fly system" and fine lighting control equipment. The production staff would include not only a stage director (usually the theatre teacher) but also a hired choreographer and a music director. This mega-undertaking is at the extreme far end of a production continuum. These kinds of productions are being mounted in schools across the country.

The *New York Times* recently noted the trend in some high schools to "supersize" the school production program, citing a handful of schools that have followed this dictum. They include Castle High School in Hawaii, Shorewood High School in Wisconsin, New Trier High School in Illinois, Harry S. Truman High School in Pennsylvania, and Las Vegas Academy in Nevada. In short, elaborate school productions are not unusual. What kind of production program do you endorse?

Consider the *Into the Woods* that was recently produced in New Albany, Indiana. This production expanded the cast to forty middle and high school youngsters employing a budget of $25,000. A previous production of *Beauty and the Beast* at this same school, budgeted at $165,000, featured flying characters and motorized scenery. Like all productions at this school, situated in a community of only forty thousand, townspeople enthusiastically support their high school theatre program, the *Times* said, by volunteering to build scenery and costumes and by helping out in dozens of other ways. The director of the *Woods* production cited earlier, David Longest, was asked in a job interview if he could do the splashy musicals. That was in 1984. His answer, according to the *Times,* was a resounding "yes." If you were asked this question as a beginning teacher at an interview, what might your answer be? Why?

Moving Along the Continuum   Musicals produced without all the bells and whistles described above and musical reviews might be placed next. Somewhere in the middle is the production of a straight play with a fairly large student cast directed by the theatre teacher, designed by students or other school faculty members (or the theatre teacher). At the other end of this philosophical continuum would be student-written short plays about student concerns that are acted, designed, and directed by students and performed in an informal space for invited audiences. These examples are intended to illustrate a production continuum from highly produced works to low-tech black box productions. Productions written, directed, and designed by students, of course, can be placed anywhere along the continuum; that is, student-generated productions can be supersized, medium, or small.

Involve Students

No matter what the philosophical roots, new teachers are urged to explore play production strategies that involve the students themselves in the planning process as well as on the performance stage. These may range from producing an original performance devised entirely by a group of students to soliciting student feedback on play or musical choices to appointing student assistant directors, choreographers, and designers. There are many ways to put students at the center of production decisions; you are encouraged to explore various models as you discover what is best for the drama program at your school.

Remember, however, that you are the leader. It is possible to simultaneously encourage student ownership in a theatre program while also maintaining a strong sense of teacher leadership. As you read the following discussion, keep in mind that you are the one who will best be able to gauge which approaches to performance opportunities will be most effective in your teaching environment. If you keep your students' best interests at the fore, you will be able to navigate effectively and responsibly the many decision-making processes of production planning.

All production experiences, no matter what their philosophical basis, should support classroom learning objectives. It is possible for theatre programs to suffer from placing too much focus on public performances, competitions, or other external influences. For example, an introductory theatre class that emphasizes performance preparation at the expense of other learning objectives surely will deprive students of valuable experiences with process and context.

Censorship

The realistic theatre teacher will understand that at some point in a career of producing plays with young people, censorship issues are likely to arise regardless of whether the play or performance piece was written by a single student, a group of students, or a professional writer. More than likely, the question will be not *if* but *when.* Various school groups have encountered disappointment when a production closed as a result of protests by community members about dramatic content that was perceived as objectionable. One teacher who had encountered no problems with mild profanity in a high school one-act play experienced issues with censorship the same year with identical language in another play. The primary difference? The censored play was written by a student. Thus, teachers should realize that concerns about dramatic material will be voiced, sometimes in surprising circumstances. We urge the beginning teacher to develop an educational rationale for selecting a particular script, include the administration in the production loop, make sure colleagues know what you will produce in plenty of time to voice a reservation, and keep the parents and general public informed about what the school is producing and why.

You would be wise to check with other departments at your school, particularly English and humanities, to see what their students are reading. Or not reading. You can get a strong feel for what is acceptable (or unacceptable) by chatting with your colleagues.

Dramatic material that is perceived as acceptable in one community may prompt questions in another. A play or musical previously performed at a school may even provoke concerns when presented at a later point in the same drama program's history. Indeed, a play that seems relatively innocuous may inspire administrators or community members to express concerns, whereas material that might have appeared more controversial could be produced without incident. For instance, plays such as *Bus Stop* by William Inge and *The Philadelphia Story* by James Barry have sparked objections not because of the content of the plays. Objections were raised, instead, about the perceived morality of the two actresses who starred in the film versions of these plays: Marilyn Monroe and Katherine Hepburn.

Develop a Rationale   Theatre teachers must be prepared to address the issue of censorship responsibly. Elements that can inspire censorship of dramatic material include (but are not limited to) profanity, mature situations, violence, sexuality, and content that may be viewed as controversial, such as political or religious themes. Regardless of whether the piece is to be performed in public or studied in class, you are encouraged to consider the educational rationale for every play selection made and be able to articulate these reasons effectively.

Every school community is unique, and thus every theatre teacher will need to navigate an individual process of selecting material that provides quality theatrical experiences for young people in their particular setting. The following suggestions for beginning teachers are not offered as a prescriptive list for handling censorship issues. Rather, these ideas are proposed as possible starting points for thinking about this critical issue. The following thoughts are shared in an effort to aid you in developing a professional approach to the management of challenging situations as they may arise.

Include the Administration   When planning a season of plays, theatre teachers will want to involve the school's administration. Some schools and districts require administrative approval of play selections; other teachers opt to involve administrators voluntarily. (It is important for the teacher to maintain the professional theatrical expertise—the approval process should not become a forum for administrators to choose performance material they like for personal reasons.) You may want to point out any particular issues in a script that might raise concerns. It is better to make another choice before a production gets underway than to deal with difficult issues later in the process, especially for those teachers new to the profession and/or to a particular school.

Distribute Scripts   You may want to provide scripts and/or librettos to department chairs, principals, or other individuals in administrative roles. The further in advance these materials are shared, the more useful the dialogues can be among colleagues.

Be Proactive   If the teacher(s) and the administration agree that the educational rationale for producing a potentially controversial script is sound and worthy for their particular environment, they may want to take proactive steps to avoid later concerns. One teacher, presented with a high school senior engaged in a directing project that involved mature subject matter, chose to communicate educational responsibility and to build community trust before the auditions took place. Scripts were made available to interested students and parents prior to auditions. The student director wrote and shared an articulate essay describing the play's theatrical and historical significance, and asked those students who auditioned to complete forms with parent signatures that expressed understanding of the play's content and consent to the young person's potential involvement. Although this advance process might not work in every setting, it was key for this particular student director's successful experience.

Inform the Public   Know the audience that may be likely to attend a play and publicize accordingly. A drama director in a kindergarten through twelfth-grade school regularly communicates on flyers and Website postings which productions are appropriate for small children and which plays are geared toward older audiences only. This communication builds a sense of partnership and mutual awareness among the families and school community members.

Learn More   Educate yourself about how censorship affects theatre education. What kinds of issues have other teachers encountered? What strategies have been successful for those teachers? What hasn't worked well? Approaches to becoming informed can range from professional research in current journals to informal (and highly useful) conversations with other theatre teachers in the same school district.

The primary goal in dealing with censorship issues is to avoid taking teacher and student attention away from the purpose of theatre in the classroom: to learn and grow through theatrical experiences. Teachers can lay the groundwork for successful programs by selecting material for their particular communities responsibly and by communicating effectively. You should understand that there are times when no matter how much excellent communication and responsible preparation has been established, censorship issues may still arise. When unexpected concerns occur, you should be able to answer questions professionally and should know your support networks in a particular school or district.

Long-Range Plans for the School Theatre Program

As you move through the experiences of first-year theatre teaching, you may find yourself wondering how the choices you make during this year will affect the long-term growth of the school's production program. Regardless of what was in place before you accepted the position, eventually the theatre program will proceed upon the lines directly related to the new teacher's philosophy, experience, skills, training, personal research, and development. The teacher's ability to plan, think creatively, and pursue and use the resources available in the school and local community will have a direct bearing on the program's success and the students' growth and learning.

Two models of sample season production schedules are presented here (see Figures 6–3 and 6–4). Of course, there are many other effective ways to approach planning for a theatre program over a period of several years. The suggestions shared below *are not presented as prescriptive checklists*. Each teacher should find the best philosophical approach for a particular group of students and school environment. Rather, these sample seasons are shared as two ways among many to approach long-term planning for a theatre program. In addition, keep in mind that as you become more familiar with a group of students and a school, you may make major revisions to the approaches you initially thought might work well with regard to long-range production planning.

Model One: Sample Three-Year Production Plan		
Year 1	1st semester	Evening of one-act plays
		Schoolwide or interdepartmental project; example: joint thematic production with chorus teacher (theatre students provide poetry/prose selections designed to tie the music together)
		Observe festival/play competition
	2nd semester	Evening of original student plays and monologues or evening of one-act plays

		Observe festival/play competition
Year 2	1st semester	Evening of one-act plays
		Play festival/competition participation (using one of the above plays)
		Schoolwide or interdepartmental project
	2nd semester	Evening of original student plays and monologues or full-length play or schoolwide project
		Play festival/competition participation (using one of the one-act plays)
Year 3	1st semester	Evening of one-act plays
		Play festival/competition participation (using one of the above plays)
		Full-length play
		Schoolwide or interdepartmental project
	2nd semester	Evening of original student plays and monologues or full-length play or musical
		Schoolwide project
		Play festival/competition participation (using one of the one-act plays)

Figure 6–3 This three-year production plan has strong philosophical underpinnings. Can you describe them?

Model Two: Sample Four-Year Production Plan	
Year 1	Showcase of scenes and monologues and/or revue of musical numbers with student-written narration
	Observation of play festival or state conference activities
	Full-length play
Year 2	One-act play performance
	Play festival or conference participation
	Full-length musical
	Theatre for young audiences for local elementary students
Year 3	Student-directed one-act plays

Model Two: Sample Four-Year Production Plan	
	Full-length play
	Staged readings of student-written plays or scenes
	Arts festival: celebration of student work with band, orchestra, chorus, visual art, and dance programs
Year 4	Original performance piece devised by students (example: oral histories on a particular community theme)
	One-act play performance
	Play festival or conference participation
	Full-length musical
	Theatre reception/exhibit technical theatre student design work

Figure 6–4 How does the theoretical basis of this season differ from the one found in Figure 6–3?

Revisit Your Choices

As your career develops, revisit these philosophical questions about production goals, as well as others that you identify through your work with young people. Teachers who have taught for a number of years often find themselves reconsidering the pros and cons of various approaches to public performances. An educator who began his career by working with high school students on numerous polished, competitive, director-centered productions later moved almost exclusively toward student-generated works that emphasized devising and playwriting processes. Another teacher focused on producing large cast performances that included every student who auditioned, sometimes upward of seventy students, with scripts that would have wide popular appeal. This educator found that including at least one small cast production of innovative material each academic year offered the opportunity for advanced students to experience roles of significant depth, as well as provided the teacher with satisfying professional challenges.

Presenting student work in a public forum provides many valuable benefits as well: young people experience motivation in preparing work to share with others; community awareness and support of the drama program can grow; teachers discover meaningful ways to translate classroom learning into performance opportunities. As a beginning teacher, you are encouraged to ask yourself questions such as:

➤ What factors are important to my students in the creation of a public performance?

➤ How will I respond to the expectation of public performance in my new school?

➤ What kind of productions will provide meaningful learning opportunities for my current students with their particular backgrounds and skills?

➤ What dramatic material will my beginning students be able to share successfully with an audience?

➤ Which production strategies will enable me to provide new challenges for advanced students?

➤ How might our school community respond to this particular approach to public performance?

➤ What are the benefits of a certain kind of performance?

➤ What challenges might ensue if I choose to produce this particular play or musical?

➤ How does my school's drama budget affect the choices I can make as a beginning teacher?

➤ How do my production goals consider issues of student ownership and creative expression, whether through devising, playwriting, student directing, or other means?

EXTENSION ACTIVITIES

1. Make a list of all the factors you think are important to a teacher when planning for a production. Create another list of elements that you feel are important to parents, school administration, and community members when considering performance opportunities. Make a third list of factors you imagine would be important to the students themselves who would like to be involved in theatrical productions. Compare and contrast the lists. How might these ideas guide your thinking about production possibilities? Would you want to update these theoretical lists with practical realities as you actually work with young people and communities? Might it be useful to invite students to make and share their own lists on "what is important to me in a theatrical production experience?"

2. Discover the productions of the school in which you are likely to intern. Discuss with the class to what extent they are director-centered or student-centered.

STAY CONNECTED

This is a U.K. site maintained by the University of Exeter: www.theatre crafts.com. Browse.

HELPFUL HINTS

➤ **Sponsor Thespians**   If your school already has an International Thespian Society Troupe, maintain it. If not, contact the international office in Cincinnati about starting a troupe (www.edta.org). There are Thespian Troupe categories for high school students as well as middle schoolers. The recognition for your students and their work is a good public relations move. Also, the Educational Theatre Association offers many excellent resources and opportunities for students and teachers. If you believe a Thespian Troupe is not a good idea for your theater program, then think about starting a theatre club. Discover the procedures that are appropriate for setting up regular club meetings, accepting dues, fund-raising, and so on. Typically you need to speak to your principal, if this is a new club. The bookkeeper and/or dean of students or activities coordinator will be your best resources.

➤ **Get Scripts**   Get to know your English department chair. Often the English department has classroom sets of books that you might arrange to borrow from time to time for your students to expand their knowledge of dramatic literature.

➤ **Make a List**   Develop a wish list of items you need for productions, the classroom library, and research center. With the permission of the administration, this wish list may be distributed to all your students and their parents and the faculty, often with remarkable results.

➤ **Set a Play Date**   Create opportunities for your students to perform. Setting a date for a production and having it on the school calendar is an important goal. If your school has an annual event such as a Renaissance fair or an international festival, find out how you and your students can get involved.

7

The Teacher and School Productions—
Practical Considerations
Doing the Job

Although the previous chapter dealt primarily with philosophical issues related to school productions, this chapter will explore some of the practical considerations associated with play production in the secondary school. These include issues of copyright, space, planning, scheduling, finances, student involvement and training, the rehearsal process, performances, and finally, reflection on the production. The place to begin the practical consideration of school production, however, is with the administrative arts coordinator.

Work with the Arts Coordinator

In a school district that has spent time developing arts programs throughout its schools, there probably will be an arts coordinator. This person can be a great resource for the new teacher. For example, if the theatre position includes a stipend for producing plays during after school hours, the arts coordinator would be able to

> ➤ share the district's expectations about numbers and/or types of productions
> ➤ convey viewpoints about participation in play festivals or competitions
> ➤ communicate a clear picture of what is expected at the district level

If the school district does not have an arts coordinator, the school's principal or arts department chair will be helpful in identifying expectations related to production philosophy.

Even if the district does not anticipate intense involvement in play production, it is very beneficial for new theatre teachers to become connected with theatre organizations geared toward secondary schools. Associating with the other theatre teachers in the district at staff development meetings, or informally, can also be very productive and informative for the new teacher.

Copyright Considerations

Producing published plays and musicals without proper licensing agreements and payment of licensing fees puts the school and the teacher at risk of injunction (stopping performances in midrun) and other legal redress in the courts. Theatre teachers, in short, should know and abide by America's copyright laws intended to protect the intellectual property of its citizens. Many industries are affected by copyright issues in today's society, such as film, music, and publishing. With recent technological innovations increasing access to copyrighted material, enforcement of intellectual property rights laws has received enhanced attention.

There are *ethical* issues as well as *legal* considerations connected with copyright law. Teachers are role models for students behavior. If the teacher and the school produce plays and musicals without proper licensing agreements, students are given wrong signals about ethical issues. For example, how can teachers ask their students to abide by other ethical restraints when their teacher flouts the copyright law? Thus, it is important for teachers to know and heed the following legal requirements.

The term *copyright* means that the authors of a work are entitled to profit from their labors. If a work is expressed in permanent form, then the author automatically owns that work. For example, if a dance is videotaped, the choreographer owns the dance. If someone writes a play on a computer and prints out a copy, that person owns the play. Others may use the work if they enter into a licensing agreement with the author. If you produce a play or musical under copyright, you must enter into a contract with the licensing organization and pay a fee, called a *royalty,* for the legal right to perform the script for school audiences, usually a flat fee per performance. Contact information for many prominent play and musical licensing companies is included in the discussion of resources in Chapter 8.

There is a popular misconception that if admission is not charged, then royalty payments are not required. This is a critical misunderstanding of copyright law. The key factor is if the production is made available to the public for viewing. There are two exceptions: *public domain* and the *fair use* doctrine.

Works in the public domain are not covered by copyright laws. Either the copyright has expired, or the author has given up copyright protection and allows the work to enter the public domain. Copyright laws have changed over the years, so determining whether or not a work is in the public domain can be somewhat complicated. At present, a new U.S. copyright is valid for the life of the author plus seventy-five years. Although certain companies will offer for production plays in the public domain, most musicals and plays are covered by copyright laws and a license must be negotiated with the author's designated agent.

Many classic plays in English, including Shakespeare's canon, are in the public domain. Classic plays in other languages may be in the public domain, but the translations often are covered by copyright laws. For example, Richard Wilbur's verse translations of Molière's works are covered by copyright laws; his verse versions are not the original versions in French.

Fair use means that teachers and students can judiciously copy materials or produce plays in a classroom setting without breaking the law. However, fair use does not mean that it is permissible to make photocopies of scripts for performances rather than purchasing them from the publishing company. A student may make a copy of material for his or her own academic use. But a teacher cannot ask each member of the crew and cast of a production to photocopy the script that is being produced. Scripts and librettos must be purchased or rented from the publishing company. If a teacher produces one-act plays or scenes for class use, then fair use allows forgoing licensing and royalty payments. But if they are produced for an invited audience, even in a classroom, the material must be licensed and a royalty paid, even if no admission is charged.

Space Considerations

Challenging and meaningful productions do not necessarily depend on the technical capabilities of the space in which they are presented. Instead, successful presentations depend heavily on the teacher's ability to use what is there and to make innovation count. Strong acting, clear transitions, rhythmic shape, and dramatic clarity do not depend on the venue.

Although some schools have well-equipped proscenium theatres, others will not have a traditional theatre space. Don't be disheartened to discover that your new school has only a cafetorium, that all-purpose space with a cafeteria at one end of a large room and a stage at the other end. This space, as you know, was designed for assemblies, using the cafeteria chairs for the attendees. Typically there is little lighting or sound equipment, little wing space, and limited physical access to the stage area.

A similar situation might exist in the gymnasium area, another space that is used for play productions by schools that do not have an auditorium or theatre. Again, invention is paramount if the architecture is inhospitable.

If the gym or cafetorium is too problematic for theatrical use, then explore the campus in search of alternate performance sites instead of being intimidated by an inhospitable cafetorium or gymnasium. For example, would the library media center or study hall be conducive for productions in an arena or thrust arrangement? Is there a commons or courtyard area where small productions might be held? Experimenting with the use of available spaces can be very exciting and rewarding. The students themselves may offer creative ideas about where a theatrical event might be performed.

At one school, for example, a group of advanced drama students wanted to perform a one-act play, but their school's auditorium was not available. So, these enterprising young people transformed a large classroom into a performance space, finding clever solutions to lighting, sound, masking, audience seating, and stage space issues.

No matter whether the performance space is traditional or "found," the teacher must ask the following questions.

➤ Will it be available for the theatre teacher upon request?

➤ Will use of this space for production be limited to the week before and/or the week of production? Or will its use be unlimited?

➤ Is there a theatrical facility that is used for productions across the district? Once again, though it may be excellent for play productions, this space may require reserving and may only be available for a limited time prior to production.

There are other space considerations besides the performance area. All theatre teachers should at least consider developing a storage site. Considerable economies of time and money can be enjoyed if "theatrical stock" is available for reuse. Scenic, costume, and prop items should be saved as "stock" to be recycled from year to year.

Some teachers may prefer to rent scenery and costumes, depending on the drama budget and their school's storage options. In the long run, however, it will prove to be more time- and cost-effective if the teacher adds to the theatre program's stock to some degree each year. This brings up other space-related questions when developing a space strategy:

➤ How will the production be built?

➤ Is there a scene shop that can be used to build scenery?

➤ Is there a costume building area?

Scheduling Considerations

Another important consideration in building a school production program is scheduling. Production dates should be placed securely within the school's calendar as soon as possible, ideally during the month before the first day of school. Scripts should be ordered and the royalties paid in sufficient time prior to auditions so that students may check out the scripts and read them.

When (and where) will the play be rehearsed? Although some teachers choose to rehearse only during class times, many work with students after school or over weekends. Quite often, schools rely on busses to transport students to and from school with a firm schedule, thus making after-school transportation challenging for some students. Some school districts have instituted the concept of a late bus, which provides transportation for students involved in after-school activities. If your school has no such program, then you are urged to develop alternatives.

Even if there is an opportunity to rehearse during the school day, not all cast members may be in the same theatre class. In this situation, the teacher must be quite inventive! One solution that may facilitate rehearsals is to discover if the faculty and administration would agree to allow students to meet for school-day rehearsals on a limited basis close to the production date. Another solution to scheduling rehearsals, especially if the teacher is doing a series of one-acts, is to cast one group of one-acts from a class and another set of plays from those who must rehearse after school. Again, innovation and flexibility are the hallmarks of a successful production program.

Discover if the theatre production can use the rehearsal space after school or on the weekends. In some schools, teachers may find it challenging to gain admittance to the rehearsal space outside of regular school hours. This is a question to be discussed with the school's administration as early as possible. In situations where it is not routinely feasible for teachers to have keys to the space and security codes, administrators may be willing to make special arrangements for needed weekend rehearsal access.

Consider the time obligations of your cast and crew. What other school or work commitments have they made? Sports playoffs, state music festivals, and marching band competitions are scheduled in advance and matter a great deal when coaches and teachers often share the same students and parent volunteers. In a larger community, there may be more resources available, but the need to share time, personnel, and audience increases exponentially in the smaller schools.

The planning document found in Figure 7–1, for example, makes it clear that from the first announcement of the full-length play to be produced, the process will occupy ten weeks of rather intensive work. This rehearsal schedule calls for a bit over one hundred hours to stage the play; while rehearsals are progressing, the physical production is also under way. If the teacher wants more time, then the rehearsal schedule must be extended. If the play is a single one-act, less rehearsal time will be required. The rule of thumb for a long play is at least one hour of rehearsal time for each minute of playing time. In short, if a full-length play is to be performed the second week of November, then the play should be announced no later than the beginning of the first week of September.

When planning a theatre production, the teacher must take into consideration events scheduled on the school's master calendar and the teacher's own academic planning. It would be counterproductive to schedule the performance dates opposite a significant all-school event or for technical and dress rehearsals to coincide with schoolwide testing. For these and other reasons, the teacher must collaborate with the school's activities director.

Production Planning Calendar	
Day	**Basic Steps**
1	Announce play to be produced and order scripts after securing permission. Set audition dates.
7	Plays available for student perusal.
8–13	Begin planning of set, lights, costumes, props.
14–16	Auditions; recruit stage management team.
18	Announce cast. Invite those not cast to sign up for crew work.
19–22	Post sign-up list for crews and urge students in your classes to volunteer.
23–60	Begin rehearsals.
23–60	Organize costumes, set, lights, makeup, props, sound, publicity.
65–70	Tech and dress.
71–72	Performances.

Figure 7–1 There are many ways to discover the essential steps in the planning of a play production. This one is, perhaps, only a bald outline of what

is entailed. It does, however, indicate that the process is a lengthy one that requires at least seventy rehearsal days from auditions to performance for a full-length production.

Financial and Other Resource Considerations

Financial resources should be investigated as soon as possible. Money matters, so ask at least the following key questions of the administration:

➤ Is there a theatre budget allocated by the school or school district specifically for production expenses? If not, is there a more general budget that might be drawn upon to fund productions? How much is available during the year?

➤ Is the theatre production program expected to make back all expenses from box office receipts? If so, is there an advance to pay royalties and scripts?

➤ How are supplies requisitioned? Are there special accounts or vendors that must be used?

➤ How long, generally, does it take for a purchase requisition to be processed and ready for use?

➤ How is student travel to play festivals funded?

➤ Does the teacher have free use of the copy machine for play programs and posters? Some schools, for example, have restrictions on how many photocopies a teacher may make per grading period or semester.

➤ Are theatre teachers and students encouraged to do fund-raising activities in order to produce the plays? If so, what are the procedures for doing so?

➤ Is there an existing arts or drama parent support group or "booster" club that can raise money for productions?

➤ Will the teacher have an active support group of volunteers in place from the faculty, parents, older students, local college or community theatres?

A significant aspect of exploring financial resources involves the concept of fund-raising. Schools will have different policies and approaches to this quite public activity. In many situations, programs are expected to apply for permission from the school before embarking upon specific moneymaking ventures. There are even schools in which fund-raising for individual programs is discouraged because a schoolwide fund-raising approach is taken by the school's administration.

If you decide to begin a fund-raising project as a new teacher, try to choose options that are as simple and straightforward as possible, especially during that first year of teaching. A few ideas that have worked well for some theatre programs include yard sales, buffet dinners, marketing ads in programs, candy sales, and selling ads to be printed on the back of drama T-shirts. Should you be in a position to conduct fund-raising, ask other theatre teachers what kinds of projects have worked well in your community in previous years, and be sure you have administrative support before launching a project.

Directing Considerations

Once you have fully committed to directing a full-length play, you are ready to consider the six logical steps inherent in any directing project. You must

➤ select the play

➤ analyze and research the script

➤ conceive the production as it will appear on your stage

➤ cast the play

➤ rehearse the production

➤ evaluate the production experience

This six-step process is not particularly difficult if the proper planning goes into each phase of production. The directing process is, however, time-consuming. You and your students will become artisans and crafters charged with making something new from scratch—a one-of-a-kind product that will be unlike any other production of that particular script.

What follows is very condensed. A full semester-long course would have to be allocated for a complete description of the directing process. If you are looking for production experience that might be equivalent to directing in a high school situation, join your campus's all-student production group where all duties are undertaken by students; this experience will be more akin to your production experiences in a secondary school situation.

1. Selecting Material   Consider many factors when selecting material for students to perform in a public presentation, including such issues as censorship, cultural diversity, and gender, among others (refer to the discussion in Chapter 3 concerning diversity and gender). Choosing performance material also connects with the teacher's previous experience and skills. Has the new teacher taken a course in stage directing or previously directed a play? Depending on the teacher's particular theatrical background, musical theatre, improvisation, straight plays, or the development of original works might take precedence in selecting the first performance piece to pursue with students at a new school. If the teacher is skilled in the technical aspects of theatre, he may find it a challenge to use his skills in an environment that is less sophisticated than the one in which he was trained. However, such situations can spark wonderful opportunities for creative collaboration with young people through teamwork and problem solving.

If the theatre teacher finds that she will be working relatively independently to create a production season, involving others on the school's staff can be a useful goal. For instance, theatre teachers might want to find out which plays the English or language arts faculty will be teaching. Some may be very appropriate for student performance. *The Miracle Worker* by William Gibson, *The Glass Menagerie* by Tennessee Williams, and *Our Town* by Thornton Wilder, for example, are commonly found in secondary literature books or on the reading lists. Of course, there are numerous other choices as well. Consider selecting one of the plays found in the school literature books or on the reading lists as a way to draw attention to the play's production as part of the school's academic mission.

The choice of specific plays to be produced will have a strong impact on theatre student experiences during the school year. Theatre teachers must consider which students and other significant personnel will be available as they select a season of production opportunities. The new teacher is advised to be conservative when selecting plays for production. Even theatre teachers who have enjoyed years of recognition and respect have occasionally found themselves in embarrassing situations because of play choice and/or casting decisions. Every community is different, and the theatre teacher may need to consider shaping performance material choices accordingly.

The most important factor to consider in choosing material to produce is the students themselves. Think about ways you might incorporate the students' voices in the process of making decisions about performance opportunities. For example, teachers with experience in creating original works might choose a theme to explore with students who devise their own scenes, write monologues, choreograph movement or dance pieces, research oral histories, or compose music for a dramatic performance. There are many production options beyond selecting a published play to direct.

One teacher in a new school devoted a number of class sessions to reading published plays by young playwrights with her students; the class completed extensive evaluation assignments for each play and, after a series of discussions and written responses, chose the two one-act plays to be performed that semester. The evaluation document used to guide the written responses for this play selection project can be found in Appendix B.

A similar example involves a teacher who chose four one-act plays and met with students on a volunteer basis during weekend hours to read, discuss, and vote on which play to produce with their drama program. It can be surprising how many students will commit to a voluntary experience such as this when they perceive that their opinions matter. The key for the new teacher is to make choices that are comfortable and realistic within the teacher's experience and are also appropriate and meaningful for the students.

2. Analyzing Structure and Discovering the Play's Background   Before rehearsals begin, the director must discover the theatrical nature of the material she has selected for production. The script should be read and reread to discover the play's beginning, middle, and end. Part of this analysis includes establishing where the climax of the play occurs. The given circumstances should be noted and studied. The script should be broken into French scenes so that rehearsals can be efficiently organized. The characters must be examined in detail to discover not only who they are as individuals but also their dramatic function (why the playwright put them in the play). Superobjectives must be fashioned for each of the characters in order to help the actors develop credible characterizations and to aid the director in shaping the production. A statement of core meaning must be crafted. These tasks are a beginning point for analysis. Your directing class training, most likely, will have provided you with the skills to analyze the script in far more detail than outlined here.

3. Conceiving What Will Be Onstage   What the audience sees and hears onstage during performance will be shaped by the actor-audience relationship of the performance space. The first step in this process is to devise a ground plan that embraces the action of the play. How and where the characters exit and enter, the arrangement of the furniture (in an interior set) or the placement of set pieces (in an exterior setting), and the special requirements of the script (Is a closet needed? Must there be a fireplace?) are all part of an effective ground plan. If the ground plan is carefully and thoughtfully devised, the blocking will almost take care of itself. If the ground plan is ill considered, then blocking will be a difficult process.

The director must plan for sound effects whether they be environmental sounds (rain, wind, and the like), imaginative sounds heard only by a certain character (the pounding of a human heart), or music to set the mood or cover scene changes. How these sounds are to be located and recorded affects the planning calendar.

Once the ground plan has been established, the "look" of the production must be established by the director. This task is often preceded by the director developing a concept or metaphor that describes the "feel" of the production and establishes the fictional world of the play. The following questions will help guide the development of the production concept/metaphor:

➤ What is the mood of the script? Happy? Sad? Nostalgic? Angry?

➤ How can this mood be translated into a visual statement?

➤ Is the script realistic? If realistic, to what extent? Or nonrealistic? How abstract? How theatrical?

➤ What is the emotional world of the play?

➤ How can the world of the play be visualized onstage?

➤ What are its colors? Its lines? Its shapes?

Once these questions are satisfactorily answered, the ground plan can be transformed into a scene design. The design of properties, lighting, and costumes can also go forward.

4. Casting Your Students On- and Offstage   As you contemplate the various factors that affect the choice of a play to produce, you will want to give greatest emphasis on how the students themselves will be involved in the production. Much of what happens in the classroom should be able to be transferred, at least in some degree, to the stage. Informal classroom performances and research or design projects can serve as springboards toward more formal performance opportunities. In fact, you should consider using the pending production as a stimulus for projects that students might accomplish in class that also can be used as part of the actual inception of the production.

Questions to think about when considering how to involve students in the production process include the following:

➤ Will the play's cast and crew be comprised of students from one particular class or drama club?

➤ Can any student at the school audition for a production?

➤ Is there an expectation, whether the school's or the teacher's, that all students who audition will appear onstage?

➤ How will technical crew positions be assigned?

It is important for each student to experience every aspect of theatre production to truly appreciate the process of making theatre. All students are not equally comfortable on stage. Some prefer, after other options have been explored, the leadership, technical, and management positions that a production offers them. If you are creating a production team of students with little or no stage or technical experience, you may prefer to set up technical interviews with interested students who are not actually cast in the production. These interviews can serve to explain what will be expected for each position. If there are older students who have previous experience, the selection of technical personnel may be easier to achieve.

Once you have determined how to approach student involvement in a production, you must consider how the cast will be selected. In some situations, such as a devised original work or a class project, these decisions may be very informal and may emerge naturally from a group's work. In many circumstances, theatre teachers hold formal auditions when students share a prepared piece, read from the script, present musical selections, or other activities.

Communication with parents about their child's participation in a school production is a very important step. By casting a son or daughter you also obligate the family to accommodate rehearsals, technical days, final rehearsals, and performances.

Examples of an audition letter and form are included in Appendix A. Depending on your school's program and policies, you may want to add a notice if it is possible that not everyone will be able to perform in the play as actors. Some teachers invite other performing arts instructors or qualified local theatre professionals to help with auditions; others conduct auditions independently. Whatever the case in your situation, you must make sure students know how casting decisions will be made and communicated. Many teachers post cast and crew lists in a common area; others prefer to share casting and crew decisions in a more private way, such as through individual letters or notices to each student.

5. Rehearsing the Production   The rehearsal process is a complicated one, embracing as it does at least six different aspects: table work, in which the actors and director analyze the script and come to a common understanding of the production's goals; blocking, in which the director makes clear through movement and staging the relationship between characters, lines are learned, dramatic actions are shaped, and the production is intensified. In this intensification stage, the director and the actors work on discovering playable objectives, making appropriate acting choices, and shaping the rhythms of the production. Finally, there is the polishing stage, in which both the actors and director discover what needs to be done to deliver a fully realized production. Following this process are the technical and dress rehearsals, culminating in the first, opening night performance.

Whereas this process has been greatly abbreviated in the previous paragraph, this fifth stage of rehearsal is the most satisfying for the actors and the director. But there is a caveat. If the actors don't know their lines, their dialogue, then the process is sidetracked and becomes a rehearsal about remembering what comes next. It means the production is in trouble, as the director and the actors can't work on the dramatic thrust of the play.

Here's a word of advice: If it didn't work in rehearsal, then it will not work in performance. Final rehearsals should be devoted to polishing the production, not remembering what comes next. Establishing the importance of actor memorization is an important task of the director.

While the production is in rehearsal, the director (also in this situation, the producer) must coordinate with a student committee on ticket sales and establish a front of house staff to recruit ushers and to develop lobby displays. Also, a student committee should be working on programs that are accurate and that promote the play production program in the school.

If you have found satisfactory answers to many of the questions asked previously, the rehearsal process will likely be more manageable, since you will already have crucial information to guide your planning. Once the play is cast, teachers will want to send written communication to parents and students that may include rehearsal schedule, theatre program expectations, and other matters that are important for the successful creation of a production. A sample rehearsal communication document can be found in Appendix A.

Whether you are rehearsing a play within a class period, during a designated drama club time, after school, on weekends, or all of the above, organization is the key to a successful rehearsal period. If students know what to anticipate and can rely on the expectation that every rehearsal will be productive, their motivation and commitment will increase.

6. Reflecting on the Production Experience   People who attend live theatre productions do not necessarily understand how many hours of hard work are involved. Only those who are actually part of the process have a clear understanding of how much real labor and time is expended in preparing a production. The teacher must be prepared to educate a school community about what is involved in any given production. Does the school have a newspaper or a television show that is sent to each classroom on a specific schedule? Students describing their personal experiences in acting and/or technical roles might create some interest in and understanding of the significance of the multiple elements of a theatrical production.

Theatre teachers will benefit from considering how they can work with students to maximize the learning opportunities from performance experiences. Some young people will encounter anxiety or insecurity when involved in the public presentation of theatrical work. How you prepare yourself and your students to reflect upon their production experiences will be a key factor in what each young person takes away from the opportunity. Questions to consider include:

➤ How will I prepare students to handle possible responses (positive, neutral, or negative) to their work?

➤ What kind of production reflection experiences will be included through opportunities such as cast and crew follow-up sessions or classroom lessons?

➤ How might the students choose to recognize their work? Is there a "production archive" in the theatre classroom that includes posters and photographs from previous plays? Is there a wall of photographs from years past to which students might add new pictures or written reflections?

The director of the production, usually the theatre teacher, is perhaps the only person who has experienced the full play production process from casting to curtain calls. So it falls upon the teacher to discover ways to share her observations about the strengths and weaknesses of the production with the production team to inspire growth and cement learning.

The feedback must be positive yet it also must identify areas for future growth. The feedback shouldn't necessarily reveal everything a professional critic might contribute but only what can lead to learning and growth. How a teacher meets this obligation depends on the individual teacher. The following suggestions are intended to help explore the issue of production feedback.

➤ Feedback should be structured for all concerned with the production from stage hands to stage manager, from actors to lighting and sound board operators. That is, just because the actors are the only people the audience sees during performance does not mean they are the only individuals who can learn and grow.

➤ Explore the audience's response to the production. Was it enthusiastic? Tepid? Why?

➤ Share with the students your areas of growth. What did you learn in the production process?

➤ Perhaps you might begin the feedback session by asking the students this question: If we had another week of rehearsals, what would you suggest we concentrate on? The unstated implication of this question is that the production (and all involved with it) was not perfect and could be improved.

➤ Ask each member of the team to share with the group what they believe was their most significant area of growth. Then ask the same participants what they believe they have to work on for the next production.

➤ Ask the actors and designers to each prepare one or two questions that will invite specific feedback from the group. This tactic will prevent unthoughtful feedback responses such as, "I thought it was great!" or "I didn't like it."

One of the most significant benefits that students can gain from meaningful reflection involves resilience. Young people who are capable of managing constructive feedback in an open and willing manner are on the path to resilience. Rather than giving up when one approach to a task does not yield the desired results, a resilient student draws on inner resources to continue learning and growing. The ability to invite feedback as a welcome experience will be extremely valuable to a young person throughout his school years and into a career.

EXTENSION ACTIVITIES

1. Choose a play or musical and create a sample rehearsal schedule. Design a scene breakdown that includes which characters appear in which scenes. Estimate how much time you think would be needed to block and rehearse individual scenes, to conduct run-throughs and dress rehearsals, and to learn music and choreography if applicable.

2. Work with a partner to design a three-year production schedule. Include play titles and authors as well as potential performance dates that leave sufficient time for rehearsals and building. Estimate a budget for each event, being sure to include items such as royalties, scripts, scenic elements, costumes, props, and publicity. Design ways to tie each production event into classroom lessons and projects.

STAY CONNECTED

Turn to Chapter 8 ("Resources for the Theatre Teacher"). There you will find the URLs for the major play leasing agencies. Most of these sites will give a brief synopsis of the script, the name of the author, the number of male and female roles, staging requirements, and royalty information. You may also request online a hard-copy catalogue from the various agencies.

HELPFUL HINTS

➤ **Know the Law**   Become very familiar with copyright and royalty laws. Go beyond the limited material in this chapter.

➤ **Participate**   Explore what theatre organizations, festivals, and conventions are available in your state or region. It is important for you and for your students to take advantage of these opportunities.

➤ **Consider Liability Insurance**   If you take students to festivals and contests or direct plays after school hours, you might consider taking out a personal umbrella policy that will protect you if there is an auto accident or some other unforeseen event that could make you liable for damages. At least investigate the extent to which your school district indemnifies you as you go about your career as a theatre teacher.

➤ **Help Others**   Consider offering to help coach students involved in the individual events segment of the school's speech and debate team.

8

Resources for the Theatre Teacher
Discovering the Possible

Imagine that you are beginning a new position as a theatre teacher. You will have taken various theatre and education courses as a student yourself. Also, your background may include numerous play productions, and you will most likely have completed some kind of practice teaching experience. Yet you may still feel that you are not ready to enter the teaching profession with confidence if you do not have a strong understanding of the resources available to theatre educators and their students. Throughout your own college or university experience, you will surely have gathered various resources that will be helpful to you in teaching theatre yourself. It is important for the beginning teacher to realize that there are diverse resources available in the field of theatre education. You are strongly encouraged to gather information from a wide variety of sources.

This chapter is not designed to endorse any particular source over another. There are other valuable resources, in addition to those described in this chapter, which can be very helpful to theatre teachers. Also, it is important to clarify that this is not a chapter of resources on specific theatrical topics or subjects; you will have gathered sources on aspects of theatre such as directing, acting, theatre history, design, and other subjects through your previous educational and theatrical experiences. The goal of this chapter is to suggest resources that are in some way of particular relevance to theatre and education. You are encouraged to use this list as a starting place and to build your own collection of resources during your career.

The single most important resource that any teacher has is the teacher's own willingness to look for new materials and ideas and to put them into use. The most successful teachers never stop learning. We hope this chapter will spark ideas for your own continued learning experiences.

Classroom Materials

You may find your first classroom equipped with sets of fine textbooks and with files and shelves of helpful supplementary materials. You might also find that you are the first teacher in your school to ever order theatre arts materials for students to use. Whatever the situation you encounter, it is important to be aware of sources for textbooks and other classroom materials. Find out what textbooks have been adopted in your state and school district; you may also find it useful to explore other classroom textbook sources as well.

Become familiar with your individual school's media center and discuss opportunities for new acquisitions with the appropriate people. Some of the companies and organizations described in other sections of this chapter also offer educational materials. For instance, the Educational Theatre Association (www.edta.org) has a Website section devoted to materials for theatre teachers and students, including items such as the *Practical Technical Theater* DVD series which explores set construction, lighting design, stage management, and much more.

You are probably already familiar with certain publishers of plays and musicals through your experiences with theatre production. A variety of publishers of dramatic material is listed in this section; you will find that some companies devote their attention to specific kinds of plays, such as Theatre for Young Audiences or new works. You might be interested in ordering anthologies that include multiple plays for classroom study, such as the Best Plays series offered through Jamestown Education. Teachers who would like an economical approach to building theatre classroom libraries may find Dover a helpful resource, as the company publishes various classic plays in "thrift editions," with some plays by authors such as Ibsen, Shakespeare, Wilde, Shaw, Sophocles, and Chekhov as inexpensive as one or two dollars per copy. You might also find e-texts useful, as various plays in the public domain are available online. For example, you may find it rewarding to adapt an e-text of a Shakespearean comedy to suit your particular cast and educational setting. (Note that this particular recommendation applies only to material that is in the public domain and should not be applied to copyrighted material.) Of course, any public performance of a play under copyright requires application for performance rights and payment of royalties.

In addition to sources for textbooks and scripts, we also include information for several publishing companies who offer collections of scenes, monologues, and other dramatic material that is worthwhile for theatre teachers and students. Note that while many of the companies listed below are devoted solely to theatre-related publication, several of them publish for other fields as well. Theatre teachers at any stage of a career will benefit from continually reading catalogs for various play and musical publishers, ordering perusal copies, reading plays as frequently as possible, and keeping a record of specific plays that might be useful for future classroom and/or production opportunities.

Glencoe/McGraw-Hill (www.glencoe.com/sec/languagearts/ theaterarts/index.html). This company publishes *Theatre: Art in Action*, *Exploring Theatre*, and *The Stage and the School*.

Pearson Prentice Hall (phcatalog.pearson.com). Publishes various theatre arts titles that the teacher may find useful as classroom reference, including *The Enjoyment of Theatre* (college intro to theatre text) and *Stage Makeup*.

Samuel French (samuelfrench.com/store/). Publishes and licenses acting editions of plays and some musicals.

Dramatists Play Service, Inc. (www.dramatists.com). Founded by playwrights, it publishes scripts in acting editions as well as licenses its inventory of plays.

Dramatic Publishing (www.dramaticpublishing.com). Publishes many scripts appropriate for young people.

Baker's Plays (bakersplays.com/store/). Offers full-length and one-act plays, as well as musicals.

Playscripts, Inc. (www.playscripts.com). Publishes and licenses many new plays.

Meriwether Publishing Ltd. (www.meriwetherpublishing.com). Offers numerous theatre texts and resources.

Anchorage Press Plays (www.applays.com) Includes plays for young audiences, as well as other resources.

New Plays (www.newplaysforchildren.com) Specializes in plays for young people.

Music Theatre International (www.mtimusicalworlds.com). One of the major resources for musical theatre.

Tams-Witmark Music Library, Inc. (www.tamswitmark.com). Another major licensor of musicals.

R & H Theatricals, a division of the Rodgers and Hammerstein Organization (www.rnhtheatricals.com). This agency publishes the Rogers and Hammerstein catalogue of musicals as well as other musicals.

Dover Publications (store.doverpublications.com). Has a line of inexpensive editions of classic plays in the public domain.

Kultur International Films Ltd, Inc. (www.kulturvideo.com). Lots of films of plays.

Professional Organizations

Membership in professional organizations can offer superb benefits for teachers. In addition to gaining practical resources, theatre teachers become part of a vast community of professionals devoted to their field. As well as the organizations described in this section, various local opportunities also exist. Beginning teachers are encouraged to seek out and explore such possibilities in their respective areas. Professional organizations committed to theatre and education and/or theatre for young audiences include the following:

American Alliance for Theatre and Education (www.aate.com) is a professional organization for drama and/or theatre educators and artists who serve young people. AATE offers a variety of publications, hosts an annual conference, and provides opportunities for artists, scholars, and educators to connect through professional networks. In addition, the organization works to develop, recognize, and support policies and standards associated with theatre arts and drama/theatre education, as well as raising public awareness about the field.

Educational Theatre Association (www.edta.org) offers many programs and opportunities for theatre teachers and students. These include publications, the International Thespian Society (honor society for theatre arts students), scholarship opportunities, professional development for educators, various programs and organizations at the state level, and an annual Thespian Festival that features numerous performances and workshops.

ASSITEJ/USA (www.assitej-usa.org) is the United States Center for the International Association of Theater for Children and Young People. This organization is devoted to the advancement of professional theatre for young audiences. Educators can benefit from the opportunities this organization presents to learn about current directions in theatre for young people.

Theatre Communications Group (www.tcg.org) is dedicated to the not-for-profit professional American theatre. TCG offers development programs for professional theatre artists and leaders, pursues advocacy, and produces numerous publications. Theatre arts teachers can gain valuable information and insight through familiarity with this organization.

Books, Journals, and Related Sources

Because the field of research in theatre education is constantly evolving, an exhaustive list of specific texts is not presented here. Rather, various publishers and other sources that offer works of interest to theatre teachers are described. Of course, there are other companies in addition to those listed here that publish useful books on theatre education. Beginning theatre teachers are strongly encouraged to visit Websites, procure catalogs, and acquire numerous current sources. Journals related to theatre and education are also listed in this section. In addition, several books that may be useful to the teacher who is beginning to build a theatre library are included here.

Heinemann Publishing (www.heinemann.com) offers various titles that explore aspects of drama/theatre and education.

Applause Theatre and Cinema Books (www.applausepub.com).

Smith and Kraus Publishers, Inc. (www.smithkraus.com).

The Child Drama Collection at Arizona State University Libraries (www.asu.edu/lib/speccoll/drama/) is a collection of books and manuscript materials on the history of theatre for youth.

Routledge (www.routledge-ny.com) publishes assorted books related to drama/theatre and education.

The Drama Book Shop, New York (www.dramabookshop.com/) offers a wide variety of performing arts materials, including scripts and books about multiple aspects of theatre.

Structuring Drama Work by Jonothan Neelands and Tony Goode. Cambridge University Press, 2000. This book explores dramatic conventions, suggests approaches to structuring drama for learning experiences, and considers "theatre as a learning process."

Theater Games for the Classroom: A Teacher's Handbook by Viola Spolin. Northwestern University Press. This text shares numerous theatre games, arranged into different categories, for use in the classroom. A CD-ROM based on Spolin's book, edited and developed by Max Schafer, is also available.

Theatre for Young Audiences: Around the World in Twenty-one Plays. Edited by Lowell Swortzell. New York: Applause Books, 1997. This anthology presents a diverse collection of plays for young people.

Stage Directing by Jim Patterson. Boston: Allyn and Bacon, 2004. A basic "how-to" directing text for the teacher who might need to brush up on directing skills. Excellent also as "in room" reference book as it is clearly written and avoids directing jargon.

Youth Theatre Journal (www.aate.com). Published by the American Alliance for Theatre and Education (AATE), this journal explores current scholarship in the field. The AATE websites says it is "dedicated to advancing the study and practice of theatre and drama with, for, and by people of all ages."

STAGE of the Art (www.aate.com). This AATE publication explores practical aspects of theatre and education.

Teaching Theatre (www.edta.org/publications/teaching_theatre.asp). Published quarterly by the Educational Theatre Association, this journal offers articles of interest to educators.

Dramatics (www.edta.org/publications/dramatics.asp). This Educational Theatre Association magazine geared toward students and teachers includes articles on various aspects of theatrical work, reviews, profiles, and new plays.

TYA Today (www.assitej-usa.org/tya.html). This ASSITEJ/USA publication shares articles exploring issues and information relevant to professional theatre for young audiences.

American Theatre (www.tcg.org). This Theatre Communications Group monthly publication explores current happenings in professional theatre, often featuring the text of a new play.

Community Resources

One of the most important steps theatre teachers can take in building a successful school drama program involves making creative community connections. There may be wonderful resources available in your local community that could be of great help to your school's theatre program. If you are familiar with the community in which you are teaching, make a list of the sources you already know in your area. What kind of connections might you pursue with people and organizations? If you are new to a community, ask advice of other local drama teachers and community theatre members. Avenues you might explore include those discussed below.

Local Theatres and Theatre Professionals   What local theatres exist in your area? Consider community theatres, church programs, secondary and college/university programs, and professional theatres. Who are the directors and designers with local theatre groups? How do these theatres find school-age actors for roles? Are costumes and scenic elements available for loan or rental? What happens to items that theatres discard when cleaning out storage spaces; are there yard sales or give-away opportunities? Do area theatres offer school day matinees and educational materials focused at secondary school students? Would directors, actors, business managers, choreographers, or designers be willing to visit your school program? Such involvement could range from a workshop for a single class to a much more extensive collaboration.

Local Sources for Supplies and Materials   What other local sources exist that would be helpful in procuring materials for classes and productions? Where are the thrift stores and similar vendors that might yield inexpensive costume and prop pieces? Are there parents or faculty members with experience in carpentry, sewing, graphic arts, or other areas that could be helpful in mounting a production? Can you buy theatrical makeup and similar items locally, or will you need to order from a distance? Are there used or discount bookstores in your area that carry inexpensive plays? One theatre teacher was able to build an impressive script library in her classroom through donations of plays from English and Language Arts teachers over a period of years. Teachers in her school knew that if they had plays they no longer taught, such items would be valued by the theatre program. Over time, this became a wonderful resource for the teacher and her students.

Local Colleagues   By looking into your state and regional organizations for secondary school theatre programs, you will be able to make vital connections with colleagues. There are other ways you can meet and learn from other educators. Start with getting to know the other middle and high school drama teachers in your district. Find out who teaches in neighboring districts, in community theatrical programs for youth, and related areas. You will find that most theatre teachers are eager to collaborate and share ideas with one another. No one understands the special challenges and unique joys of theatre education better than another teacher engaged in similar ventures! Other teachers may be able to provide you with helpful information about practical aspects of producing plays with young people, such as recommendations of rental houses for costumes and scenery.

You may find that other theatre teachers will be eager to share sources for classroom materials, loan items when possible, and offer creative ideas. For example, one group of teachers regularly communicated with one another about script ideas for their students through email, phone conversations, and informal social meetings. This professional connection included instances when one teacher might email another, "I need a great duet musical piece for a male and female student who have strong acting skills but limited musical theatre experience" or "I'm looking for a one-act that will challenge three advanced students." Numerous helpful responses would result from such queries. Although national organizations have networks and online chat opportunities that could yield similar ideas, this group of teachers found that over years of collaboration they came to really understand each other's preferences and standards. These educators enjoyed sharing the work of their colleagues' students when they came together in festival settings.

There are many more opportunities and sources that can be helpful to theatre teachers and their students in addition to those described in this chapter. You should bear in mind while using this chapter that Web addresses may change, and occasionally a resource may be discontinued or merged with another entity. Not every resource will be valued by every teacher, but it is hoped that you will find many useful sources through examination of this chapter as well as through other avenues that you find for yourself. As you explore some of the resources described in this chapter, compile your own list of discoveries as you encounter new possibilities. The extension activities that follow are designed to help you get started.

EXTENSION ACTIVITIES

1. Order plays from three or more different publishers. Create your own system for evaluating and cataloguing scripts. Organizing elements may include: cast size, technical needs, level of maturity in content, period, and genre.

2. Acquire and read books on theatre and education from the publishers described in this chapter and/or other sources you discover. Which books help you make choices about philosophical and pedagogical issues related to theatre education? Which texts aid in specific classroom teaching pursuits? Which books will be of practical use to you on a regular basis in your classroom? What texts will you consult when thinking about broader educational

issues? Is there a particular book that inspires you on a personal level? Create a system for organizing your professional library.

3. Peruse two or more different journals or magazines related to theatre and education. Identify at least one article in each of the following categories that you would like to share with theatre educator colleagues: (1) scholarly article on an aspect of research in the field, (2) practical lesson plan that you might adapt for use with your own students, and (3) review of a current book or other resource.

4. Research local theatre associations and drama festivals that provide opportunities for middle and high school students. What are the options in your area? What does each organization offer for students and teachers? Consider attending festivals and conferences on your own before taking students. Make choices about which opportunities are in line with your own philosophy and goals for your students. Are you interested in a conference that provides workshop sessions for students? Do you want the drama program at your school to compete for first-place rankings? Is it important for your students to share their performance work with other schools in a less competitive atmosphere? Are there scholarship and college audition opportunities with any local or state organizations? Inquire about the possibility of "shadowing" an experienced teacher at a festival to learn firsthand about schedules, expectations, and procedures.

STAY CONNECTED

Playbill is the company that supplies theatre programs to most Broadway and off-Broadway shows as well as to various theatres around the country. Their website offers theatre news and discounts to New York and London theatres. It's gossipy and fun: Playbill.com/index.php.

HELPFUL HINTS

➤ **Take it Easy**   Avoid the enthusiasm that often affects new teachers. Don't join every committee, although it is a good idea to make yourself available to one or two. Becoming a team player is very important. Making friends on the faculty is also valuable.

➤ **Invite the Experts**   Introduce yourself to local experienced theatre people, broadcasting professionals, playwrights, film makers, agents, and so on. Invite them to visit your classroom to speak to students about pursuing these and related careers, what is available locally, and how students can take advantage of these opportunities.

➤ **Take a Field Trip**   When you feel comfortable with your students, plan and execute a field trip to a local theatre for a tour and perhaps a performance. If possible, try to add a response session for your students with the actors and director.

➤ **Locate an Artist-in-Residence**   Plan to have an experienced theatre artist visit your school to coach your students in some special classes. Variety is the spice of life, and students often respond well to a visiting specialist.

9

Putting the Pieces Together
Communication, Collaboration, and Creation

After studying various areas related to teaching theatre, you may find it beneficial to consider the following questions: Why is theatre education important for young people? What professional and personal qualities will you bring to the teaching of theatre? Consideration of these questions will encourage you to bring together the multiple strands explored in this text by reflecting on the pedagogical and developmental benefits inherent in theatre education. As you read this chapter, consider how the benefits of theatre education connect with the theatre standards in your state (or the national standards). By addressing the standards in the classroom, how does the theatre teacher enable students to experience the learning opportunities described in the following discussion?

What Can Young People Gain from Theatre Education?

Benefits of Theatre Education   Theatre teachers often find themselves in the position of explaining the multiple benefits for students who study theatre arts. Whether in conversation with administrators, parents, colleagues, or students themselves, theatre teachers will find it helpful to consider answers to the question: What can a secondary school student gain from a theatre course? The primary focus of a theatre class involves education in the subject matter designated for the particular course, which might include various acting and directing activities, technical theatre and design, playwriting, or an introduction to theatre experience, among other possibilities. In addition to the subject-specific purposes for teaching theatre, however, multiple other benefits emerge for students who experience theatre education.

Developing the Mind and the Body   Through the study of theatre, young people develop their individual minds and bodies. Theatre students are asked to solve problems, adapt to change, and develop an interest in other people. They also practice identifying a need for certain knowledge, procuring information, and applying new knowledge in meaningful ways. For example, a student creating costumes for a play set in a specific time and place in history would identify, acquire, and apply new information in the research, design, and construction process.

Theatre also invites students to grapple with complex thought about space and time. They might perform a script written hundreds of years ago, while wearing costumes finished perhaps a week prior, with staging rehearsed over a period of months—all as if the events of the play were happening for the first time. In addition to offering opportunities for practicing different ways of thinking, theatre study can influence how students react and respond to situations. Through the often challenging processes of creating theatre, a young person may gain resilience and persistence.

Literacy skills are important for theatre students' success. Directing, acting, playwriting, design—all of these theatrical endeavors involve an element of interacting with text. Theatre study can also ask students to think and write analytically, speak articulately, learn to be specific, and support their points. Thus, theatre provides unique opportunities for building skills and heightening interest in working with text through reading, analyzing, sharing, and creating the written word.

Young people who study theatre develop their bodies in a variety of ways. Numerous aspects of theatre experiences are highly tactile and sensory. Especially for actors, theatre education may involve development of flexibility, strength, control, and the ability to use the entire body to communicate a role. Even for those students who do not focus on performance, theatre study offers ways to enhance kinesthetic ability, as in the precise and specific motor functions required to create a scale model for a set or to construct a costume.

Fostering Independence and Intellectual Curiosity   Through theatre study, young people may develop an enhanced interest in taking ownership of their own learning, as they learn with a level of physical and verbal engagement that can heighten curiosity to discover more. This kind of independent curiosity is evident in the example of a seventh-grade student who encountered summarized versions of several Shakespearean plays, explored roles in an informal setting, and wrote original monologues and dialogues based on her interpretation of Shakespeare's characters. After this series of lessons, the young person spent part of a summer reading the entire text for three of Shakespeare's comedies and tragedies, learning several sequences by heart just for fun. Admittedly, such a level of independent interest will not happen with every student, but without the opportunity for experiencing glimpses into dramatic worlds through theatre study, this kind of self-directed achievement would likely not transpire at all.

Learning with Others   The successful study of theatre invites the development of numerous social skills. In order to work in this collaborative art form, students must work with other people. Theatre students express and negotiate differences in opinion, such as verbal critiques of a performance as audience members or the group creation of a unified production design. Young people also work together in pairs and groups to identify and pursue achievable goals. In addition to learning *with* one another, theatre students may also learn *from* one another. A simple example can be seen in a technical theatre setting wherein a more experienced student (with teacher supervision) leads a small group through the process of painting a series of flats to fulfill an established set design. Theatre education builds communication skills, which offer significant benefits for young people who are preparing to pursue careers. In theatre classrooms, students learn to solve problems with others and to use time effectively as they work together in groups or teams. Theatre also asks students to develop and share their ideas, which requires skills in communication and focus.

All of the ingredients that go into creating a work of theatre—including auditions, design meetings, rehearsals, audience etiquette, and performance procedures—involve structure, accountability, reliability, and responsibility. For example, in order to find success a student must be accountable (for example, learning lines or building pieces by an established deadline), reliable (for example, regularly showing up to do what is expected), and responsible (for example, interacting as a trustworthy member of the school theatre community). The whole truly does depend on the parts; young people who participate in theatre are asked to commit to mutually respected structures and expectations.

Learning From and About Others   Theatre study offers opportunities for broader social and cultural understanding. Through various activities and pursuits, theatre requires students to think from another's perspective. The new perspective might be that of a dramatic character, a playwright, a fellow actor, or an entire group of people specific to another place and time. One example of this kind of theatrical encounter can be seen in the translation of oral history into performance. Students might create an original theatre piece as a group, drawing on oral history documents gathered through research or even through personal interviews. There are many ways that teachers can construct theatre experiences that engage meaningfully with culture and history, as well as possibly build empathy among young people.

Students are also able to make connections with communities outside their immediate classroom environments through theatre experiences. High school students can create a production for young children and either tour the play to elementary schools or invite groups to visit their school theatre. Colleges and universities may provide opportunities for their theatre departments to work with middle and high school students, ranging from student matinees of university performances to summer or after-school ongoing youth theatre programs. Students also meet other young people from different schools who share their interest in theatre by attending state and regional drama festivals. A particularly meaningful example of young people making human connections through theatre involved collaboration between an elementary school teacher and a high school theatre teacher, whose students worked together to create an original performance piece. High school students helped the younger children create and rehearse staging choices for the presentation of original work written by the elementary school students. The high school group experienced the opportunity to mentor younger students; the elementary children grew from the individualized attention of the older students. Both groups were able to actively engage in making theatre. Numerous kinds of theatrical connections exist among school theatre programs, as well as between theatre programs and other organizations; the examples included here provide a few ideas about possible collaborations. Theatre can encourage students to connect with the larger world, both figuratively through intellect and artistry and literally through collaborative efforts such as those described here.

Becoming a Theatre Artist   Most students who take part in middle and high school theatre courses will not pursue professional careers in theatre. Of course, theatre education enables students to value theatre and, more broadly, the performing arts. Students who have positive encounters with theatre as young people are more likely to engage with building performing arts communities as adults. For instance, they may work with community theatres as actors, board members, technicians, or other capacities; they may engage with arts education advocacy at the local, state, or national level; they may become loyal audience members of educational, amateur, and professional theatres in their communities. Young people who enjoy theatre may enrich their own lives and the lives of others (as parents, teachers, friends, community leaders) by seeking out ways to experience theatre as adults.

It is vital for students and teachers to recognize and value theatre as an art form in its own right. Through the study of theatre, students may also encounter aspects of multiple other forms and disciplines as they are woven together in a unique theatrical tapestry, such as movement and dance, literature, vocal music, media, design principles and visual art, various technical skills, and public relations. The mere existence of a theatre program does not guarantee the presence of all possible advantages articulated here. The vast diversity of teachers, students, and programs makes the field complex and variable. All of the benefits described thus far will not apply to every student and every program, yet theatre does offer a truly unique forum for students to embrace multiple ways of learning. Beginning teachers are encouraged to recognize the importance of the subject area itself while also looking at other advantages that may be experienced through theatre education.

What Qualities Will You Bring to Students as a Theatre Teacher?

After exploring the various topics discussed in this book, you may wonder how you fit into this picture. The characteristics of a potential theatre teacher and possible benefits experienced by those who teach theatre are not presented as a prescriptive list. However, it is useful to think about some of the qualities that the theatre teacher can be called upon to demonstrate or acquire, as well as to dwell on some of the personal gains associated with the profession.

What characteristics do you bring to the teaching of theatre? One of the most rewarding habits that a teacher can develop involves reflection. As you contemplate the benefits that theatre experiences offer to young people, you will also want to consider what characteristics you will bring to the classroom as a teacher. In thinking about these qualities, you may agree that successful theatre teachers:

- ➤ value courage and integrity in the art of teaching
- ➤ explore communication and collaboration as integral classroom components
- ➤ have a passion for theatre in various forms
- ➤ want to create theatre with young people of widely varying skills and experience levels
- ➤ derive satisfaction from organization and problem solving; examples include: crafting rehearsal schedules for students with vastly different time commitments, brainstorming low-budget sets and costumes, staging transitions with no wing space–or maybe not even a theatre space

➤ want to discover what young people express about their worlds through theatre and to help them learn about the worlds of other people, times, and places

➤ embrace change and invite students to experience change as an opportunity to learn

➤ want to build enthusiasm for theatre throughout a school and community, guiding students as ambassadors for the art form

➤ explore practical strategies for time management and for setting reasonable expectations of themselves as a teacher

➤ possess sensitivity and flexibility, recognizing the necessity of providing structure as a clear and responsible leader while also shaping collaborative opportunities for young people to experience genuine ownership in the classroom and theatre

➤ appreciate students for who they are and are becoming, identify their talents and gifts, and lead them in appreciating one another

You may also find it inspiring to consider what rewards you might anticipate as a theatre teacher. The vibrancy of theatre classroom life demands constant renewal, grappling with big questions. Although this can be draining, it also makes for exciting teaching and adventurous learning. The study of theatre requires curiosity and enthusiasm for learning about the world and other people—from both students and teachers. Theatre educators have consistent opportunities to learn more themselves as they lead young people through theatrical explorations. Theatre teachers create in collaboration with the intense, fervent force of adolescence, which can provoke healthy artistic challenges. Teachers are able to craft many different kinds of theatre with diverse young people in mutual, shared artistic expression. Theatre teachers get to know many students—fascinating, aggravating, ever changing. They also learn from adolescents how young people experience and interpret the world and how they express those ideas through theatre.

Your Own Experiences as a Theatre Student   What do you recall about your own experiences as a theatre student, at any stage in your development? You will surely have encountered various benefits from studying theatre yourself; after all, you have decided to pursue a career as a theatre educator. Perhaps you draw inspiration from your memories of working in theatre classes as a middle or high school student or from experiences as a younger child. You will most likely have also experienced important growth in your theatre classes as a college or university student. As a beginning teacher, you are encouraged to draw upon your own background in thinking about goals for working with young people.

Theatre Education: A Growing and Vibrant Field   As you move into a career as a theatre teacher, you will find it beneficial to build awareness of happenings in the field of theatre education on a state and national level. Begin now to collect thoughts—your own and those of other educators and students—on why young people benefit from theatre experiences. Remind yourself of the unique qualities you bring to the field as a teacher and as an artist. Teaching theatre is a rewarding and exciting profession; take advantage of the resources available to you, and take pride in the important goal of adding your voice to the field of theatre education.

EXTENSION ACTIVITIES

1. The purpose of this activity is for the beginning theatre teacher to articulate and present reasons for the importance of theatre classes to any student. Look at several of the Websites that follow (or similar sources); focus on areas such as advocacy and research. Create a persuasive presentation on the significance of theatre education in a format (for example, PowerPoint or a brochure) that could be accessible to a variety of community members at any school. Practice giving your presentation for different audiences; ask your listeners for questions and use their responses to guide further research in strengthening your work.

2. Make a list of the different kinds of benefits you feel that you experienced through your own background as a theatre student. If possible, create separate lists for different periods in your development, depending on your individual history. Try to be as specific as possible in your recollections. Compare your list(s) with other students in your class or group. What similar responses did you all encounter? Where might your background be unique? Write a personal reflection on how your history as a theatre student yourself will affect how you approach working with young people as a theatre teacher.

STAY CONNECTED

The following Websites will connect with professional organizations that will help you discover more about the field generally and the value of theatre education specifically.

American Alliance for Theatre and Education (www.aate.com)

Educational Theatre Association (www.edta.org)

Arts Education Partnership (www.aep-arts.org)
    Kennedy Center Alliances for Arts Education Network
    (www.kennedy-center.org/education/kcaaen/)

HELPFUL HINTS

➤ **Collect Your Own Resources** Explore your community for secondhand bookstores. Building a classroom library and research center is an expensive process. Finding useful books at reduced rates extends your budget.

➤ **Learn About Financial Procedures** Get to know your school bookkeeper. Make her an ally. Find out how you can spend the money the principal may have allocated to the theatre program in the annual budget. Learn the procedures for accepting and disbursing funds and follow the rules to the letter.

➤ **Explore Local Theaters** Investigate your community for local theater companies. Community theaters often give students opportunities to usher and attend productions for free. Colleges and universities sometimes have special student performances and rates. Professional theatres frequently have intern or apprentice opportunities for the serious student.

Appendix A
Sample Audition and Rehearsal Communication Documents

The following sample audition letter, audition form, and rehearsal document were adapted from communication sent to middle school parents and students; they could be modified for use with older students as appropriate for a particular program. Information that would change depending on the production, school, teacher, and time frame is italicized and capitalized for ease of adaptation.

These documents were designed for after-school rehearsals and voluntary student participation. Teachers working with a class of students in which everyone is required to participate in a production would need to modify such documents to reflect their program goals. In addition, different teachers will have different concerns. Some of the policies and expectations expressed in these samples may not work for every teacher, student, or school. Thus, it is important to decipher what is best for your environment and adapt your approach as you learn over time. For instance, the procedures regarding athletic schedules and involvement of coaches described in the documents below were developed by a teacher who encountered numerous conflicts and communication issues with students committed to many activities.

Also, consider how you can involve your students in designing their own theatre policies and expectations, such as the sample list found at the end of the rehearsal packet below. If young people have a voice in building a program, they will be more likely to feel ownership and embrace expectations about theatre space, safety, and respect.

Sample Audition Letter

Dear Students and Parents/Guardians,

Our first middle school play production of the *DATES* academic year will be *NAME OF PLAY* by *PLAYWRIGHT* to be performed on *DATES* at *PERFORMANCE TIMES*. We are going to have fun and learn a lot during the rehearsal and performance process for this play. Those students who wish to audition are advised to read the following information carefully and return the attached form to me no later than *DATE*.

Auditions will be held on *DATE* and *DATE* from *TIME FRAME* in the auditorium. Students should identify an audition date on the attached form.

During the auditions, students will participate in vocal and physical activities and will read several roles from the play. Students do not need to prepare an audition piece in advance for this particular production.

So that the rehearsal schedule may be designed effectively, please fill out the attached schedule of availability. I will design the rehearsal schedule based on the information provided through this form. Although it is understood that unforeseen emergencies do arise, a productive rehearsal process requires commitment to a clearly negotiated and mutually respected schedule.

If you have any questions, please do not hesitate to contact me at *EMAIL ADDRESS* or *PHONE NUMBER*. I look forward to sharing an exciting and rewarding year of theatrical endeavors with you and your student.

Sincerely,

NAME OF TEACHER

Sample Audition Form

This form, with signatures, is required for students who plan to audition for *NAME OF PLAY*. Please return to *NAME OF TEACHER* in *LOCATION* by *DATE*. Thank you!

AUDITION DATE (please circle):   *DATE*   OR   *DATE*

Student name: Grade:

Parent/Guardian Name(s):

Phone: Email:

Previous Experience
The auditioning student may describe previous drama/theatre experience and education on the back of this sheet if desired. However, please note that no previous experience is necessary to audition.

Schedule Availability
Please list on the reverse all early morning (before-school), after-school, and weekend time frames when the student *is available* to rehearse.

Are there any particular dates the student would not be available for rehearsal as communicated above? If so, please write them on the reverse side.

Required Signatures
(Student's name) is available according to the information communicated above for rehearsals from *DATE* to *DATE*. If cast, the student agrees to fulfill the commitment to this production in whatever role assigned by the director. She or he would be available for the dress rehearsals from *TIME FRAME* on *DATES* and for evening performances on *DATES*. If the student is involved in athletics or another after-school commitment, the coach or sponsor's signature is provided here to communicate agreement with the above schedule availability.

_____

(Parent/Guardian Signature)   (Date)

_____

(Student Signature)   (Date)

_____

(Coach/Sponsor Signature If Applicable)   (Date)

Sample Rehearsal Communication

NAME OF PLAY by PLAYWRIGHT
NAME OF SCHOOL DRAMA PROGRAM

Dear Cast/Crew Members and Parents/Guardians,

Thank you for your commitment to the rehearsal and performance process for this exciting theatre experience. Please take time to read every document in this packet carefully and to ask questions early so that we can prepare effectively for our production. I look forward to working with you this year.

Sincerely,

NAME OF TEACHER

How to Read This Rehearsal Schedule

Identify your role(s) and scene(s). Look carefully at the rehearsal schedule and highlight all dates and times for every scene in which you appear.

Double-check your work. Saying "I didn't read the schedule correctly" is not an excuse for missing rehearsal. If you have questions about the schedule, ask now!

If you are absent from school because of illness or emergency, you are expected to call (or ask your parent/guardian to call) or email *NAME OF TEACHER* to notify her that you will be absent from rehearsal. The only conflicts that will be excused are those previously noted on audition forms. With a cast of this size and a production of this complexity, it is vital that everyone arrives to rehearsal *on time* and ready to concentrate for the entire rehearsal period. Students should make sure well in advance that coaches/sponsors of other activities are aware of rehearsal and performance times.

In the event that severe illness/unavoidable emergency arises and a cast member is unable to attend a performance, she or he or a family member should email or call *NAME OF TEACHER* as soon as possible.

Drama room phone = *PHONE NUMBER*

Email = *EMAIL ADDRESS*

Cast and Crew

[List roles and performers along with technical positions and names of students fulfilling these responsibilities.]

Rehearsal Schedule

[Provide scene breakdown, including page numbers and characters appearing in each scene. Be sure to include technical meetings as well as scene rehearsals. If students are to provide any of their own costume pieces, include a description of what is required and when it is due. Be as specific as possible. For example, if all of the costumes are being rented, borrowed, or made, but the students are expected to provide their own shoes, describe what kind of shoes are needed and ask students to begin wearing them during the rehearsal period. Or, students may be asked to provide all of their costume pieces, depending on the requirements of the play and the drama program budget. Whatever the case, the earlier this information is communicated, the easier preparations will be later in the process.]

[Communicate daily and weekly rehearsal plans. A sample design is as follows. (Note that the following information is shared to help you get started in designing a rehearsal schedule. Of course, an actual schedule would unfold over a number of weeks or months and would include many more meetings!)]

Day and Date	Time	Scenes to Be Rehearsed or Characters, If Individual Work Is Planned
DAY/DATE		"Off book"—all lines should be learned by this date
DAY/DATE		Costumes due in drama room (if applicable)
DAY/DATE	Time	ALL: Run through entire play
DAY/DATE	Time	Technical crew rehearsal
DAY/DATE	Time	Dress rehearsal
DAY/DATE	Time	First performance
Actor call:	time	
Crew call:	time	
Curtain:	time	
DAY/DATE	Time	Strike set, costumes, and props

Theatre Policies and Procedures: NAME OF SCHOOL

Safety Students are in the drama room or the auditorium with a teacher on the premises at all times; students are not outside or elsewhere during rehearsals and performances.

Students are asked to avoid the following

- ➤ running in the aisles
- ➤ pulling, moving, or otherwise handling any curtains or backstage items unless instructed
- ➤ any other action that could compromise the safety of an actor or crew member

Exiting the stage into the audience should always be accomplished by using the stairs on either side of the stage.

Respect During rehearsals, students will watch quietly, read a book, or do homework in the audience seats while not onstage.

Only the prop manager/backstage crew or the actor who uses a particular prop/costume/set piece should handle the item.

Students will demonstrate respect for contributions made by all cast and crew members.

Space Water in a closed container is the only drink permitted in the auditorium or drama room; no food, please.

All scenery and other items stored backstage that are not directly involved in the production are off-limits.

While backstage in the drama room during dress rehearsals and performances, students will clean up after themselves and bring homework/reading material to occupy offstage waiting time.

Thank you for abiding by these important guidelines. If you have ideas for revisions to this list, please submit your observations in writing to *NAME OF TEACHER.*

Appendix B
Response Form for Play Selection

Response Form for Play Selection

Student Name _____ Date _____

Name of Play _____

Playwright _____

Please complete one of these response forms for each play you have read. Your written observations will be taken into account as choices are made for the evening of one-act plays this semester. Be as specific as possible and back up your opinions with points about the particular play. If you need more room, then use the other side of this form.

Cast Size and Breakdown   Would the number and gender of roles available provide sufficient opportunities for our drama student population? Comments:

Perceived Dramatic Quality of Script's Communication and Theme   What do you like (or not like) about this play with regard to theme? Communication of characters and dramatic action? Comments:

Realistic Production Needs   Can this production be mounted for [BUDGET FIGURE] or less? Remember to consider all royalties, scripts, costumes, props, set, publicity, and other expenses. Comments:

Projected Expenses

Royalties	$_____
Scripts	$_____
Set	$_____
Costumes	$_____
Props	$_____
Publicity	$_____
Other (describe)	$_____

Appropriateness of Script for School Community   Is this script suitable for our school community? Why or why not? Comments:

Potential Challenges   What potential challenges might arise in the production process for this play? How might those challenges be resolved? Comments:

Numerical Ranking   Overall, rate this play as a choice for our drama program on a scale from 1 to 10 (1 = lowest, 10 = highest). Please circle a number below.

1   2   3   4   5   6   7   8   9   1 0
Not suitable   Somewhat suitable   Very suitable

Appendix C
Rubric: Resource Portfolio for the Beginning Theatre Teacher

Name of Student

Criteria	Level 1	Level 2	Level 3	Level 4
Organization	Not a particularly useful document for future reference: arrangement appears random; table of contents missing or not useful; not divided into appropriate sections	Mostly easy to use and/or read: arrangement usually not logical/ clear; table of contents incomplete; haphazardly divided into appropriate sections	Fairly easy to use and/or read: arrangement usually clear/logical; table of contents is missing some entries and one or two are not fully descriptive; usually divided into appropriate sections	Very easy to use and/or read: arrangement clear/ logical; table of contents is descriptive and complete; divided into appropriate sections
Completeness	Much appropriate material is not included	Some appropriate material included but some is missing	Most all appropriate material included	All appropriate material included
Presentation	A sloppy presentation unbecoming of a professional; hard to access	A bit ragged and worn and inconvenient to use	Neat and professional but some problems with appearance; fairly easy to access	Neat and professional; easy to access
Supplementary materials	Few, if any supplementary materials	Some appropriate supplementary materials in some areas	Many appropriate supplementary materials presented in most areas	
Mechanics (grammar/spelling)	Grammar and spelling errors noted	Writing is grammatical and correctly spelled		

A total of 17 points can be earned, one for each level of accomplishment.

Score: 17 = 100%   16 = 94%   15 = 88%   14 = 82%   13 = 76%   12 = 70%   11 = 64%

Index